The Financial Banana Split

The Financial Banana Split

Financial Literacy From High School To Retirement

Bruce A. Rowland, LNHA

This edition revised June, 2022.

Banana Split Marketing LLC
516 South Dixie Hwy. #330
West Palm Beach, FL. 33401
www.FinancialBananaSplit.com

This publication is designed to provide a basic understanding of general personal finance. No professional advice or services is being given to the user of this publication by the publisher or author, including legal, financial, insurance, real estate, or any other matter. Before any actions in these areas are taken, or if advice is required, the services of a competent professional person operating in the field of interest should be sought. Publisher and author assume no responsibility thereof.

Note to reader: As of the publication date of this book, every attempt has been made to provide you with current information. Laws, regulations, interpretations, and meanings of words, phrases, and numbers are subject to change, and their current status at time of use should be verified.

Full disclosure: Some of the links in this book may be affiliated links, and the publisher may earn a commission if you purchase through them. This disclosure is pursuant to federal law (FTC).

Library of Congress Cataloging-in-Publication Data:

Rowland, Bruce A. 1956 -
The Financial Banana Split / Bruce A. Rowland

ISBN Paperback: 978-0-9993704-1-4
ISBN eBook: 978-0-9993704-3-8

Ordering information: Discounts available on quantity purchases. For details, contact the publisher.

Printed in the United States of America

Contents

INTRODUCTION

ACHIEVE FINANCIAL LITERACY

INTRODUCTION

1

Book's Purpose and Goal

This book's ***PURPOSE*:** **To Put you in control of your financial life.**

This book's ***GOAL:*** **To help you achieve the American Dream!**

The American Dream is owning your own home – mortgage free – and having enough income from investments to retire- at whatever age. Not work your entire life just to pay bills.

With smart money management and avoiding bad financial decisions - all explained simply in this book – even a modest, steady income can lead to the creation of great wealth over time.

Most people believe these financial fairy tales about themselves:

1. I'm not **lucky** enough to accumulate wealth.
2. I'm not **smart** enough to accumulate wealth.
3. I'm not **talented** enough accumulate wealth.
4. I don't know where to **begin** to accumulate wealth.

NONSENSE!! Here's the truth about why **you are able** to accumulate wealth:

1. You're **lucky** enough because now you possess the proper tool – this book.

2. You're **smart** enough if you read 10th grade-level books.
3. You're **talented** enough if you follow the material in this book.
4. You **begin** your financial journey with this book.

If you don't know how to control your money, those who do know how to control money (people & entities), will eventually control you.

How To Use This Book

1. Read, review and understand the material in this book.
2. Use this book as a reference. Refer to it before you make major financial decisions such as home, car or stock purchases and any of the other many financial subjects covered within.

Additional Learning Experiences

Our website: www.financialbananasplit.com contains three more areas to help you on your financial journey:

1. ***Gain Money Self-Awareness*** Emotions and money don't mix! Understanding and empowering your emotional relationship with money to be positive and logical helps you avoid making bad money decisions. This website section tells you how.
2. ***Collaborate For Wealth Building*** You don't have to go on your financial journey alone! Many others are at the same stage financially. Done smartly, you can achieve the American Dream sooner with a little help from your friends / investment partners. This website section tells you how.
3. ***Our easy-to-play board game:*** **Ice Cream and Money – For Everybody!** reinforces The Financial Banana Split book. *Buy it – Play it – Learn it – Earn it.* Buy it on our website.

2

Ice Cream Makes Me Happy

At the moment you sink your mouth into a sweet, creamy, scoop of ice cream . . . your eyes close, and your nostrils widen as you deeply inhale the sweetened air below. Your mind drifts into the soft cloud of a happy daydream.

It can be a simple vanilla soft serve enjoyed outside a drive- up window on a hot summer day or a complex scoop of bourbon-infused banana ice cream with dark chocolate ribbons, flecked with pieces of honey-glazed toasted almonds, eaten in front of a roaring fireplace on a dark and stormy night.

These words easily transport us to a positive, comfortable place because the language of ice cream is familiar and understood – not the least bit frightening.

This book's goal is to make your relationship with money positive, comfortable, familiar, and understood – not the least bit frightening.

This will enable you to more strongly pursue the American Dream:

Home Ownership and Financial Security

3

True Story - Employee

Can you achieve the American Dream if you start with nothing? Here's a true story illustrating that, with the right mindset, you can!

While I was operating a facility as a licensed nursing home administrator (LNHA) in the Bronx, NY, a longtime employee came to me in tears.

She told me she'd been evicted from her apartment along with her young son and her sister's asthmatic child. She asked if I could somehow help her regain her residence.

Her job was steady, with good pay and benefits, but her boyfriend had "borrowed" several months of rent money and she had been evicted for non-payment. I called the sheriff's office but was told back-rent charges had to be paid in full before the housing authority would remove the door locks.

Since young children were involved and she was an excellent employee, I offered a loan through the business to repay her debt ($3,500) if she agreed to automatic payroll deductions until the loan was paid back in-full. She agreed.

She and the children returned to their apartment and she got rid of her "boyfriend."

The loan was paid back in full and on time.

Later, I learned she had never stopped the automatic payroll deductions I'd set up as her employer. She and I were ahead of our time with the simple, now widely accepted wealth-growing technique known as automatic deductions – we just didn't know there was a name for it.

After implementing these automatic deductions, she must have made adjustments to her lifestyle (budgeting), because she was also able to fund a savings account. Before I left the business and New York – over 20 years ago – she told me she had saved over $5,000 dollars.

Moral of the Story

If a victimized, urban, single mother of two – broke, in debt, and evicted from a public housing project – can pull herself together, learn to budget, and accumulate thousands ($) ...

SO CAN YOU!!

ACHIEVE FINANCIAL LITERACY

Definition:

Financial Literacy is the ability to understand and use financial tools.

Overview

1. **Ingredient One – The Dish: Cash Flow and Banking**
   The foundation: solid, no leaks.
2. **Ingredient Two – The Banana: Home Ownership**
   The defining structure of the Banana Split and the American Dream.
3. **Ingredient Three – Ice Cream: Loans/Credit/Debt**
   Ways to use money are as numerous as ice cream flavors.
4. **Ingredient Four – Toppings: Avoiding Financial Landmines**
   They cover other ingredients and affect their overall flavor.
5. **Ingredient Five – Whipped Cream: Investing for Wealth and Early Retirement**
   Rapid growth showcases your determination to follow financial plans and quickens your pace towards the American Dream.
6. **Ingredient Six – Cherry On Top: Goodwill and Charity**
   It's sweetness gives your finances direction and purpose.

Ingredients 1 - 4 protect your money. Ingredient 5 grows your money. Ingredient 6 gives you emotional support.
Together they guide your finances throughout life's stages.

1

Ingredient One: Cash Flow and Banking

Cash Flow and Banking are the dish in the banana split. It's the part of your financial plan that has to be solid, no leaks.

Being aware of and actively managing your cash flow is the difference between controlling your money or your money controlling you . . . period.

How much you spend on credit cards, entertainment, food, clothes, or telephone and how much you're able to save need to be informed choices because they tie-in directly to your cash flow.

Credit and debt are so impactful to your financial health that they're covered separately in Ingredient Three: Loans, Credit, and Debt.

A budget helps you make informed choices because you'll realize how much available cash you have to spend each month before overspending into debt – explained below.

A friend recently asked me: "How does someone blow through a million dollars without realizing it and end up broke?" My answer:

"They didn't pay attention, didn't know or didn't care about cash flow: how much was coming in versus how much was going out."

This scenario famously happens to celebrities all the time.

My Point: If a millionaire superstar can get into financial trouble, **you** must be **aware** of your **cash inflow and outflow**, which is exactly what a budget helps you see.

What causes you to spend beyond your means? Advertising. There's nothing wrong with you. You're human. Advertisers know this and use it to sell you products and services, attempting to prioritize their need to sell over your need to carefully consider before buying.

We fall victim to advertising with strong psychological appeal. Advertisers use behavioral science (the study of behavior) and data gathered from our smart phones, credit card transactions, etc. to understand our buying habits.

They know us better than we know ourselves. On our website, in the section Gain Money Self-Awareness, you'll learn techniques to understand and redirect your actions from those with negative outcomes to positive outcomes for your financial future.

You can also resist these ever-present, sophisticated techniques that don't add lasting quality to your life and move you further away from the American Dream with the following techniques:

Cash Flow Defense - Four Helpful Techniques

(Explained on our website and in this book)

1) Use your Power Money Mantra (From our website): Gain Money Self-Awareness, to control potential bad spending choices.

After going through this sequence a few times, it becomes automatic. You'll apply it to all future purchasing decisions.

2) Start saving for your future now, whether to buy a home or to increase retirement savings to counter overspending. A simple way to accomplish this is by implementing automatic deductions from your paycheck or checking account and transferring these funds into savings/pension/investment accounts. This uses the "out of sight, out of mind" technique (detailed later).

Automatic deductions are a major stepping stone on your path to financial security. This is so important it's detailed again separately in Ingredient Five: .... and was the method used in True Story-Employee, above.

3) Be a "Conscious Consumer." Earning money takes your time and effort. Have respect for yourself and consider your spending choices in view of this.

You have a lot more control over what you spend . . . than over what you earn.

Before you open your wallet and hand over your money, ask:

- Will I really use this product or service? Is it worth it?
- Can I live without it? How does this change my life?
- Do I own anything else that provides the same use?
- Did I feel a need for this item before I saw it in the store?
- Can I get the same product or service for less elsewhere?

4) Be aware of and track your cash flow using a budget. A sample one-page blank budget is provided on the next page. It's simply adding up all your income and then adding up all your expenses and subtracting one from the other. The net result shows if you spend all, more, or less money every month than you take in – the basic cash flow concept. Elsewhere in this book are techniques to improve your monthly cash flow by helping you save and grow your wealth.

You can also go to: www.FinancialBananaSplit.com to download apps for services that help you develop a budget and track and manage your money.

These apps allow users to keep track of activity from banks, credit cards, investments, loans, and financial transactions through a single user interface. Users can also create budgets and financial goals.

Feel free to use my format to input your own information. You're looking for realistic numbers – a good guess – not perfection. Your accuracy improves as you complete each monthly budget.

Obtain information from your bank and credit card statements, receipts, checkbook, cash on hand, memory, etc. Looking back on how you spent your money every month will amaze you. It's a real eye opener into your spending habits.

Also, make a list of once-a-year expenses (birthdays, holidays, etc.), add them all together, and divide by twelve. Put this amount in the "Annual Expenses" item of your monthly budget. If you don't spend this amount monthly, you'll have it to spend at the time of year it was meant for: holidays, birthdays, vacations, etc.

YOUR MONTHLY BUDGET

BUDGET EXPENSES	COLUMN 1	COLUMN 2	
Rent or Mtg + Prop. tax	$ ___	Insurance	$ ___
Utilities	$ ___	Clothes/shoes	$ ___
TV/internet	$ ___	Education	$ ___
Phone	$ ___	Student loan expense	$ ___
Car expenses: gas/ins/pkg/maint.	$ ___	Loans: other	$ ___
Salon: hair care/nails, etc.	$ ___	Dry-cleaning	$ ___
Pharmacy	$ ___	Cosmetics/skin care	$ ___
Entertainment	$ ___	Health insurance	$ ___
Travel/vacations	$ ___	Hobbies/sports	$ ___
Food: groceries/delivery, etc.	$ ___	Childcare/sitter	$ ___
Kids' allowance/other expenses	$ ___	Pet care	$ ___
Subscriptions & club dues	$ ___	Charity	$ ___
Down-payment: future house	$ ___	Child support	$ ___
Emergency fund: future house	$ ___	Alimony	$ ___
Pension/Investments	$ ___	Credit card minimum	$ ___
Annual expenses	$ ___	Other	$ ___
COLUMN 1 TOTAL	$ ___	COLUMN 2 TOTAL	$ ___

Expenses: Column 1 + Column 2 =

TOTAL BUDGET EXPENSES: $ ______________

BUDGET INCOME	COLUMN 1	COLUMN 2	
Net salary(s)/wages	$ ___	Child support	$ ___
Bonus/other	$ ___	Alimony	$ ___
Cash income (tips, etc.)	$ ___	Net investment Income	$ ___
Net refunds (tax, etc.)	$ ___	Odd jobs/hobby	$ ___
Net rental income	$ ___	Other	$ ___
Net other	$ ___	Other	$ ___
COLUMN 1 TOTAL	$ ___	COLUMN 2 TOTAL	$ ___

Income: Column 1 + Column 2 =
TOTAL BUDGET INCOME: $ ______________

TOTAL BUDGET INCOME minus
TOTAL BUDGET EXPENSE =

YOUR MONTHLY BUDGET NET AMOUNT (+/-): $ ________

Whatever your monthly budget net amount is, you can increase your surplus or decrease your deficit (so it becomes a surplus) by conducting a basic review of your expenses. Decide which are needs (necessities) and which are wants (desires). Be smart – trade several wants for savings.

The most powerful way to cut costs is to plan your purchases.

Monthly Budget Transfers

Surplus money should first go into your Emergency Fund (4-months living expenses). Then into your home as a Down-payment Fund or early mortgage payoff. Then into your pension. Then into your non-pension investments.

The easiest way to do this is to implement automatic deductions from your checking account monthly or from every paycheck.

Example: If your take-home pay is $800 dollars every two weeks, have your employer deduct $112 ($8 per day x 14 days) and automatically deposit it into your savings account. Or instruct your bank to transfer twice this amount monthly from your checking account into your savings account. Then transfer into appropriate account.

It's "out of sight, out of mind," and there are no weekly/monthly decisions to be made about whether or not, or how much, to deduct. It keeps these monies out of easy "spending cash" reach. You'll adjust your lifestyle to accommodate to this automatically (Automatic deductions are detailed later in Ingredient Five: Investing).

An alternative to a bank is a program offered by the Social Security Administration, part of the federal government. Their free program invests your money in United States Treasury bonds, considered one of the world's safest investments. You can withdraw your money at any time – penalty free. Downside? Slow growth at low interest rates. www.FinancialBananaSplit.com for a link to this website.

Divorce – Special Note: Money issues are the biggest single cause of divorce. Divorce – a huge roadblock to the American Dream. **Develop** a sample monthly budget **now** with your potential mate that you can both agree upon – **before** getting **married.** Work out money issues now before they cause problems.

Banks - A Big Part of Your Cash Flow Picture

Definition: A bank is a financial institution licensed and regulated by the government as a Receiver of Deposited Monies. Banks operate as commercial banks or credit unions. Corporate shareholders own commercial banks. Depositors, as members, own their credit union.

Credit unions generally have lower fees for banking services, lower loan rates and higher interest savings plans.

Commercial banks are more business friendly and offer a greater variety of services.

Deposit insurance: Your money – up to $250,000 per qualified account – is insured against losses arising from a bank failure.

Commercial banks use the Federal Deposit Insurance Corporation (FDIC), and credit unions use the National Credit Union Association (NCUA). They are equally safe programs.

Verify that your bank participates in one of these (there is usually a sign on the door) by asking for proof of membership.

Choosing a Financial Institution

Bank accounts include checking and savings accounts, money market accounts, Certificates of Deposit and IRA (Individual Retirement Accounts) pension accounts.

Access to banks and credit unions can be made by visiting a physical location (branch), ATM machine, or online by computer or by using your smartphone.

Use the following criteria to choose the right bank for you:

- Convenience: Do you want or need to interact in person? Then choose a bank with a physical location near you.
- Ease of Transactions: How will you conduct your business? In person? Online? Using an app to make deposits by smartphone? Using nearby ATMs? Choose a bank that best fits your lifestyle.
- Interest: Who pays higher rates on financial products: Savings, CD's (Certificates of Deposit), checking, money market, etc.
- Fees: What fees are charged for what? When? Credit card? Checking accounts? How many free checks can you write a month? Is there a minimum balance required to avoid a monthly fee?

Basic Bank Accounts

Name/Type	Purpose/Explanation
Checking Account	Used for spending. Little or no interest paid. Access: checks/debit card/electronic transfer/bank deposit and withdrawal slip at bank. Penalties for overdraft (spending over your account balance) and fees for service/too many checks per month or keeping too low a balance. Checking + Savings =Total balance.
Savings Account	Used for saving. Interest paid as a percentage of your average savings account balance:

	2% = $2 per year on a $100 balance. Access: bank deposit and withdrawal slip/ electronic transfer. Service fees/ minimum opening deposit/low balance fee.
Certificate of Deposit	Referred to as a CD. Used for savings. Has specific duration: 1 year, 6 months, etc. Pays higher interest rate than savings account. No access for duration/term of CD. Penalties for early termination. Don't use for monies needed before CD term ends.
Money Market Account	Used for savings. Higher interest rate than savings account. Interest rate changes based on the market interest rate. Access: checks and electronic transfers. Minimum balance required to open and maintain - if not, fees charged.
Individual Retirement Account (IRA) Pension	Used for retirement savings and growth. Many investing options - see Ingredient Five: Investing for Wealth and Early Retirement. Access: electronic bank transfer / withdrawal slip. Penalties for early withdrawal = before age 59 ½.

Banks may offer other services including: mortgages, home equity loans, car loans, personal loans, credit cards, wire transfers, foreign currency exchange, safe deposit boxes, traveler's checks, money orders, etc. Visit bank or website.

How To Open A Bank Account

1. Visit a bank in-person or on-line: www.Bankrate.com/banking.
2. Documents you will need for each person applying include:
   a) Valid government-issued identification: passport/driver's license, etc.
   b) Social Security card, Trust Account tax ID/ or other Valid Federal tax ID #.
   c) Proof of current address: driver's license, utility bill, property tax bill, etc.
3. Complete + sign the bank's application. If under 18, parent/guardian needed.
4. Applying may not require funds. Opening the account will. Minimums vary.

Balancing Your Checkbook

1. What it is: Comparing your financial records to the bank's records for your checking account. And verifying both ending balances match.
2. Why do it? To see your current available balance, catch bank errors and merchants and identify fraud – the earlier the better.
3. When to do it: Once-a-month. Monthly = less work and better accuracy.
4. Do I need to do it if I only bank on-line? Yes – for the reasons above.
5. How to balance your checkbook:
   a) Record all transactions in your checkbook register or on-line spending tracker whenever you make a payment with a check, debit card, electronic transfer, bank withdrawal or deposit slip

or any other deduction or deposit into or from this account. Record the check #, date, payee, purpose and amount.

b) Update your checkbook balance every time you make a transaction.

c) Reconcile the bank statement with your check register/spending tracker:

1. Review your bank statement line-by-line. Place a check mark in the box of your check register by the check or other deduction or addition which corresponds to the one on the bank statement.
2. Start with the ending balance of your bank statement.
3. Add any unchecked register deposits to the balance.
4. Subtract any unchecked register deductions from the balance.
5. The above steps 2+3+4 should equal your current checkbook balance. If they don't equal: a) Review your checkbook for accuracy. Did you miss any deposits or charges? b) Any fees missed? c) Did you receive refunds from returned items or missing shipments you wrote down but the bank doesn't know about? d) Are there any charges that are not accurate or purchases you don't recognize? This could indicate FRAUD! e) Contact the bank and/or the merchant or credit card to clarify or dispute any unknown charges **immediately** - see Disputing Incorrect Billing Statements, below. Contact the fraud unit of any of the above if you suspect fraud and ask for a letter or e-mail as proof of your interaction with them. Follow steps for identity theft in Ingredient Three if you suspect you are an identity theft or fraud victim.
6. Mark your check register at the point where you ended for the month.

Checks

Review the following components of a check and proper check writing procedures with teens:

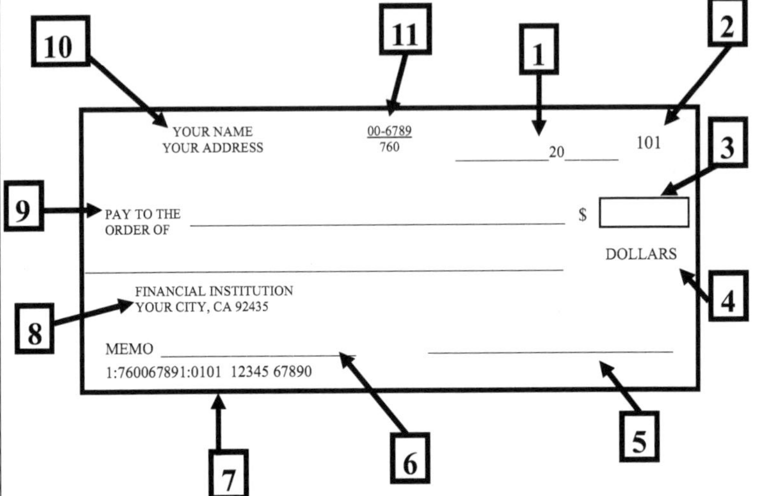

1. **Date**: A check must include the date that it is written
2. **The check number** is used to record and track each check and its amount
3. **$:** The amount of the check written in numbers
4. **Dollars**: The amount of the check written in words
5. **Signature Line**: A check is valid only if it's signed
6. **Memo**: An area to note what the check was for
7. **Computer routing numbers**: The bank and state routing numbers and account number written in magnetic ink that can be read by a computer
8. **Bank name and branch** that handles the account
9. **Pay to the Order of**: The name of the person or company the check is for
10. **Name and address of account holder**
11. **Routing numbers**: The top numbers are a code for the state in which the bank is located. The bottom numbers name the regional Federal Reserve Bank that will handle the check

Checkbook Register

CHECK NUMBER	DATE	DESCRIPTION OF TRANSACTION	AMOUNT OF PAYMENT (-)	AMOUNT OF DEPOSIT (+)	BALANCE FORWARD
	2/1	**Balance**			**$2000.00**
	2/2	**ATM Withdrawal**	**300.00**		**1700.00**
	2/3	**Monthly Service Fee**	**10.00**		**1690.00**
321	2/5	**Tom's Ticket Printing**	**138.50**		**1551.50**
322	2/7	**C & P Cola**	**250.50**		**1301.00**
	2/9	**ATM Withdrawal**	**83.00**		**1218.00**
323	2/10	**Sun Community Center**	**350.00**		**868.00**
324	2/10	**Tony's Catering**	**407.00**		**461.00**
	2/14	**ATM Withdrawal**	**103.00**		**358.00**
325	2/19	**Trophy Center**	**97.75**		**260.25**
	2/25	**ATM Deposit**		**635.00**	**895.25**

Reconcilement Worksheet

CHECKS OUTSTANDING- NOT CHARGED TO ACCOUNT

Check Number	Check Amount
# 324	**$407.00**
Total	**$407.00**

Bank balance shown on this statement	**$667.25**
Subtract checks outstanding	**$407.00**
Total	**$260.25**
Add deposits outstanding	**$635.00**
	$
	$
Balance	**$895.25**

Should agree with checkbook balance after deducting service charges or other charges not in your checkbook (if any).

BANK STATEMENT

MONEY T@LKS
111 Main Street
Anywhere, USA 12345

Period ending	2/23/XX
Date of last statement:	1/25/XX
Account:	123456789

Talent Scouts
50 State Street
Anywhere, USA 12345

Date	Item	Check Amount	Deposit Amount	Balance
	Opening balance			$2000.00
2/2	ATM withdrawal	$300.00		$1700.00
2/3	Monthly Service Fee	$ 10.00		$1690.00
2/5	Check #321	$138.50		$1551.50
2/7	Check #322	$250.50		$1301.00
2/9	ATM withdrawal	$ 83.00		$1218.00
2/10	Check #323	$350.00		$ 868.00
2/14	Withdrawal	$103.00		$ 765.00
2/19	Check #325	$ 97.75		$ 667.25

Check#	Amount
321	$138.50
322	$250.50
323	$350.00
***	
325	$ 97.75

*** denotes missing check

Previous Balance	Total Deposits	Total Checks	No. of Checks	No. ATM Trans.	No. of Deposits	Service Charge	New Balance
$2000.00	$0	$836.75	4	3	1	$10.00	$667.25

Disputing Incorrect Billing Statements

1. Assemble and review all related documents (paper/computer) to find all information related to the issue: billing statement, bank and credit card statement, invoice, cancelled check, contract, etc. Find your account number.
2. Compare incorrectly billed amount to your assembled documentation.
3. Write down the discrepancy: correct vs incorrect amount and on which documents this information appears.
4. Contact the seller by phone, e-mail or USPS and explain your findings.
5. a) Seller proves there was no mistake – you agree – okay – end.

   b) Seller understands and agrees and promises to correct: ask how/ when.

   c) No seller response or you're not satisfied with explanation:

1. Ask to speak with a supervisor. Still unacceptable?
2. Contact Federal/state consumer protection agencies per Consumer Protection Laws- Finance, below.

Consumer Protection Laws - Finance

The purpose of consumer protection finance laws is to prevent harm to consumers (the general public) caused by predatory business practices including: mortgages, credit cards, car loans, personal loans, debt collection, housing discrimination, student loans, fraud reporting, securities investment fraud, privacy of personal financial information, telemarketing, identity theft, credit reports, scams, deceptive pricing practices, deceptive advertising, etc. Your best protection is full disclosure of all terms and conditions, clearly stated.

Consumer protection laws are overseen by the federal and state governments. Contact them for information about your rights, questions and to file a complaint.

Federal Trade Commission (FTC): (877) 382-4357 / consumer.ftc.gov.

A state's consumer protection agency: (844) 872-4681 / usa.gov/state-consumer.

True Story - My Consumer Complaint

Several years ago, I received an on-line quote from a moving company for a Florida > Colorado move, for $1,500. I signed a contract Estimate. They picked-up my belongings and moved it to their warehouse. When I relocated, I called the company to ask them the status. They told me the price was $11,000 dollars to ship belongings to Colorado. I thought they mixed my move up with someone else's – they hadn't. They were serious. I noticed at the bottom of my contract a complaint number to call for the Federal Department Of Transportation (DOT).

I called and told them my situation. They said I could register a complaint but suggested the quickest solution was to call the movers back, tell them I spoke with DOT and see if they were willing to work with me to resolve this issue. So that's what I did. As soon as I mentioned DOT the movers immediately apologized and asked: "Didn't our manager call you back about this mix-up? (Yeah, right!) They reduced their price from $11,000 > $3,500 (reasonable) - The End. Moral of the story: You have rights and power as a consumer. Use them to your advantage.

True Story – A Million-dollar Bank Error

I briefly became a millionaire when I was twelve years old due to a banking clerical error.

When I was growing up in the suburbs in the 1960s, most people banked with their local bank. Adults had checking, savings, and Christmas accounts, and children put part of their birthday or holiday money in little passbook savings accounts. A passbook looked like a passport. Each time you made a deposit or withdrawal the amount was posted into your passbook on a typewriter by a bank teller. One day I made a small deposit into my passbook savings account and then went home and put the passbook away in my bedroom dresser drawer and promptly forgot about it.

The next day the telephone rang – most people had only one telephone in their house, generally hanging on the kitchen wall. Our phone was the standard olive green, rotary dial. My mother answered. She became highly excited from whatever the person on the other end of the line was saying.

She asked me, "Bruce, did you make a deposit with your passbook at the bank yesterday?"

Being a boy, I assumed I must have done something wrong. I sheepishly replied, "Yes," and my mother said, "Go get it and bring it down here right away!"

I got the passbook and gave it to my mother. She opened it and exclaimed, "Oh my goodness . . . you're right!" She quickly hung up the phone and showed me my little savings passbook. Instead of posting the total as $100 dollars, the bank teller erroneously posted the total as $1,000,000!

I was rich!! . . . for about 24 hours.

My mother instructed me to go to the bank right away where the embarrassed bank teller corrected her error. She put lines across my newfound million dollars and replaced it with the proper $100. Moral of the story: Check every detail of your bank and credit card statements every month. Just because it's on a statement doesn't mean it's true – you need to protect your money and credit and be the judge … good and bad!

Ingredient One - Conclusion

Cash Flow and Banking are interconnected and is the most important Ingredient to understand and regularly monitor for your financial health.

Ingredient One: Major Points

1. Cash Flow Management = Control your money- don't let it control you.
2. A Monthly Budget shows your cash inflow versus your cash outflow. Many banks have phone apps for monthly budgeting use.
3. Automatic Deductions prevent overspending=increased savings / less debt.
4. Develop a budget before marriage or to help before divorce.
5. Bank choice: Ease of use, charges and fees, interest rates earned/ charged.
6. Review and balance your bank statement monthly for errors and accuracy.
7. Evaluate if certain spending is a need or simply only a want.
8. Balance your checkbook every month

9. Dispute incorrect billing charges. Take immediate action for suspected fraud.
10. Know your consumer rights and how to exercise them.

2

Ingredient Two: Home Ownership

Home Ownership is the banana in the banana split. It's the foundation of a banana split and the foundation of the American Dream.

Purpose of This Book

The purpose of this book, as I've mentioned, is to enable you to achieve the American Dream, which includes home ownership.

Goal: Rewrite your STORY . . . and unlock your DESTINY.

Your Story

Your story (or that of your child/grandchild) may include one or more of these truths:

- You can't afford a home with your current job.
- You're burdened with student debt.
- You'll never have the financial flexibility to retire.

Home ownership is the key to rewriting your story and unlocking your destiny because real estate historically rises in value, which gives you:

- A wealth increase that doesn't require another job.
- An asset you can borrow from to pay off student debt.
- An additional income stream – renting all or part of it.

A statistic from the United States Census Bureau reveals the average new home cost $82,500 in 1981 and $242,300 in 2011 – an increase of $159,800 and a 300% gain. This period reflects the term of a standard 30-year mortgage.

My parents bought our family home in 1958 for $36,000. It was a medium-sized split-level design – standard suburbia. It sold in 1998 for $405,000 – a $369,000 increase and a gain of almost 1200% in 40 years.

These examples illustrate long-term home ownership. Sometimes shorter periods have proven disastrous for homeowners, such as the mortgage meltdown of 2008. In this case, a house price decline of 75% from its high was not unusual. People lost everything. But it was a great time to buy a home if you could afford it, as my friend June did in True Story – June Chopper in Ingredient Five. I discuss timing considerations for house buying, below.

Catch up/Step up

Problem: You can't afford to buy a home because you can't save enough money to catch up to ever-increasing down payment requirements due to student loans, etc.

Taking action by implementing this book's recommendations now makes it possible to become a homeowner with much less cash and income than you thought possible. This puts increasing home values in your favor.

Home Ownership - Quick Overview

A primary purpose of this book is to for you to become a homeowner able to pay off your mortgage sooner than later.

A mortgage is the type of loan used when buying a home.

"Home" refers to the real estate you own and reside in regardless of type: house, condominium, co-op, townhouse, etc.

Home ownership lets you progress from having dreams to making plans, because it stops you from being victimized by ever-increasing rents.

A fixed-rate mortgage on your home (the interest rate never changes) can even decrease if you refinance when interest rates decline (detailed later in this Ingredient).

After you pay off your mortgage your housing costs decline dramatically because you no longer have monthly mortgage payments. Owning becomes much cheaper than renting.

Owning your own home, mortgage free, is primary financial security because it makes cash flow available to invest towards wealth accumulation (detailed in Ingredient Five: Investing).

On the path towards owning your own home you'll be able to accomplish other important financial goals too:

1. Increase Your Wealth – Home values historically increase over time. Your home ownership percentage also increases as you pay down your mortgage principal every month.
2. Save for Retirement – Cash saved by not paying rent and put to work in pensions and other investments can grow by themselves (see Ingredient Five: Investing).

3. Pay off Student Loans – Your house is an asset that can be used as collateral to secure a home equity loan at a lower interest rate than your student loan. Calculations for assessing your best loan options are described later in this Ingredient.

Home Ownership -- Your Basic Financial Pathway

Your basic financial pathway to home ownership uses a "step up" approach, as follows:

Save to become part-owner and then buy your own home:

- Save enough money to purchase a "share" in a collaboratively owned house. You become a shareholder (like a corporate stockholder) while living in this house with others.
- Sell your share later for a profit. Use this as down-payment money to buy your own home. The profit is tax free if used this way – the IRS considers it a "residential rollover."

Example

This is an example of how to follow Home Ownership – Your Basic Financial Pathway:

Example based on house purchase price of $200,000/down payment 10% ($20,000)/your ownership percentage 25% (¼).

1. $8 a day x 365 days = $2,920 (amount saved in one year).
2. $2,920 x 3 years = $8,760 (amount saved in three years).
3. Amounts needed for your 1/4 house ownership:
   $5,000 – Mortgage down-payment.
   $2,275 – House emergency Fund (explained later).

$1,485 – House closing costs (explained later).
$8,760 – Total amount needed = Total amount saved.

4. The house value rises $100,000 in five years from $200,000 to $300,000. Your share = $32,275: $7,275 (Refunded down-payment + house Emergency Fund) plus $25,000 (Your share, 25%, of the $100,000 increase in the house's value).*
5. You sell your share and walk away with $32,275 cash.
6. Use this money towards a down-payment on your own home.

* Plus additional monies paid off on mortgage

A Word about Crowdfunding

"Crowdfunding," has become popular recently and is used by individuals and companies to raise money for projects, especially start-ups, when capital isn't available through traditional channels (banks, etc.). If you're planning on obtaining a mortgage, a traditional lender won't issue you one if you've borrowed money for your down payment, including crowdfunding.

It's possible crowdfunding could be a source for the down payment if the right deal is offered. The crowdfunding participants might insist on a share of the profit when you sell your house share. This defeats the purpose of the "step up" process for home buying and should be kept in mind when evaluating any offer. Also note interest rate and structure offered: fixed/variable/balloon? (All explained later.)

Comparisons to current mortgage interest rates and crowd-funding websites: www.FinancialBananaSplit.com.

Home Buying Basics

It's important to understand home buying basics to prepare for and evaluate your home buying readiness and get the best deal.

There are eight home buying basics to understand before buying a home either as a shareholder or as the sole owner(s).

1. Legal

A deed in your name(s) equals property/home ownership the same way a title gives you ownership of an automobile.

Your specific rights and responsibilities can include:

- Quiet enjoyment of your property.
- Inviting who you want, when you want, to your house.
- Remodeling, demolition, construction to fit your lifestyle.
- Selling or renting your property and making a profit.
- Paying property taxes. Buying fire and liability insurance.
- Maintaining your home's exterior within locally accepted standards for safety, sanitation, physical appearance, etc.
- Loss of use due to disaster or construction defects.
- Your county clerk will have information on taxes, etc.
- Does a home owners association (HOA) exist? Applicable fees and restrictions? Check zoning regulations before remodeling.

2. Investment

Owning your own home should be your initial primary financial investment because of all of its financial benefits.

As an investment, your home incorporates many classic investment strategies (detailed in Ingredient Five: Investing):

- Appreciation: Real estate historically increases over time.
- Wealth Creation: You increase your percentage of home ownership with each mortgage payment because this reduces the outstanding principal owed on your mortgage balance (except "interest only" mortgages, explained later).

- Pay Yourself First: Paying off your mortgage benefits you first, not a landlord.
- Cash Flow: Deductions for mortgage interest, property taxes, home office, etc. all decrease your annual tax bill, adding to your positive cash flow.
- Asset Diversification: Your investments should be "diversified" – put into different "classes" of assets: stocks, bonds, real estate, commodities (oil, corn, soybeans, etc.). This protects your money because, when some asset classes are down, others are up. Your home is your primary real estate asset.
- Leveraging: Using other people's money to make money. The majority of money for your house purchase is loaned to you by the mortgage lender. You only contribute the down payment cash: 5% to 20%. Example: House purchase price = $200,000. Your down payment = $20,000 (10%). You obtain a mortgage for the other $180,000 (90%). Purchasing a $200,000 house with $20,000 cash is 10:1 leveraging of your money.

3. House Affordability

How much home can you afford to buy and maintain? To obtain a mortgage, you must be able to pay all your basic monthly housing costs, known as PITI – see below.

"PITI" (pronounced pity) covers the house costs of Principal + Interest + Taxes + Insurance. The total should not exceed 28% of your monthly household gross (pre-tax) income. Also, taking a larger loan, even if offered, can and has put people at greater risk of foreclosure, as happened in 2008. Example: Total gross monthly household income = $4,200. Total monthly PITI expenses should not exceed $1,176 (28% of $4,200).

Components of example:

a) $180,000 mortgage @ 3.49% (P+I)/per month =	$807.28
b) $3,000 annual property taxes/per month =	$250.00
c) $1,200 annual homeowner's insurance =	$100.00
Total PITI/per month =	$1,157.28

In the above example, the monthly income qualifies to buy this house because it's more than the monthly PITI: income of $1,176 versus PITI of $1,157.28.

Your PITI affordability level: www.FinancialBananaSplit.com

Affordable Housing

Our nation has an affordable housing crisis due to factors such as lack of supply – only 20% of new housing is classified as affordable (National Association of Home Builders). Luxury apartments are favored by builders. A potential solution for many is the "step up" collaborative home ownership program advocated throughout this book. This works best for those seeking three- to five-year housing partners who want to: buy > profit > move up to sole ownership.

Let's look at the following information:

The average monthly rent for a one-bedroom apartment is $1,057.

Compare this to the previous monthly PITI example. Realizing your own house can give you thousands in income tax deductions every year (equal to your mortgage interest plus property taxes) plus the historical price appreciation of real estate, it's clear owning is a better value than renting.

Additionally, if this house is collaboratively owned by four shareholders, each shareholder's monthly PITI is $289. Compare that to the average one-bedroom apartment rent of $1057 – wow!

That's an even more compelling financial reason to own your own home sooner than later.

This example is illustrated on our website in Collaborate for Wealth Building. That details how to become a homeowner sooner than later – with a little help from your friends.

Other housing-related costs to consider beyond PITI include:

- Utilities: power, water, sewer.
- Internet, television, and phone services.
- Lawn maintenance and snow removal.
- Repairs, maintenance, replacement, improvements as needed.
- Private Mortgage Insurance (PMI) if down payment > 20%.

4. Risks in Home Ownership

No investment is risk free and home ownership has its own unique risks:

1. Price declines due to economic conditions locally or nationally. You will be most affected if you must sell when prices are much lower than your purchase price. Renting your house or your share in your collaborative house might be your only option until prices appreciate enough to sell.
2. The house is uninhabitable, temporarily or permanently, due to damage from a natural disaster, mold, or structural failure. You're still liable for mortgage payments and real estate taxes. Insurance might pay for all or part of your loss and expenses. You'll need to temporarily or permanently relocate.

Take these risks into consideration, as well as all the benefits of home ownership, and try to determine your probable future scenario before making this major life commitment.

Buying a home at a price close to its historic low rather than its historic high with a mortgage you can afford can significantly reduce your financial risks and improve your investment outcome.

5. The Mortgage

The Federal Truth In Lending Act (TILA) requires your lender to give you two documents itemizing all mortgage financing costs: Initial: Loan Estimate Form (3 pages). Final: Closing Disclosure Form (5 pages). Samples: FinancialBananaSplit.com.

Your best choice for financing is the standard 30-year fixed-rate mortgage loaned at a competitive interest rate. This is because the mortgage payment is fixed and can never go higher, giving predictability to your monthly payments. It also has the advantage of going lower if you choose to refinance when interest rates decline. It's the gold standard for a reasonably affordable mortgage.

Note: Be aware, **refinancing** a mortgage means starting over with a **full new mortgage term**. Prepaying your current mortgage in a shorter time rather than refinancing might be a smarter choice and might also save thousands in additional interest. See example below.

Verify there is no prepayment penalty. Then you can make extra principal payments when you have extra cash. Your own fully paid-off residence is generally the smartest investment you can make. Why? Live where you don't own and you're paying someone else's mortgage and taxes for their property.

Example: House price of $200,000 with mortgage of $180,000 @ 3.49%: 30 year mortgage total cost = $290,621. If paid off in 20 years, total cost = $250,932.

This early pay-off is done by paying an extra $230 per month towards the mortgage. That's a $39,689 savings in interest payments.

A paid off mortgage greatly increases your cash flow! Income, credit rating and down payment determine a mortgage rate, points (a fee) and type offered: fixed/variable/blend/interest only.

The variable rate mortgage changes when market interest rates change. May be unaffordable if rates change from low>high = risk.

Caution: If you don't qualify for a 30-year fixed rate mortgage, maybe wait. Disaster ahead if you lose your home in foreclosure: ruined credit and 7-year wait to qualify for a mortgage.

Example: The "interest only" mortgage. Your monthly mortgage payments are low because they only go towards paying the interest expense on the mortgage, not principal.

The risk with this type of mortgage is that eventually you have to pay off or refinance it, typically in five or ten years, in one lump sum known as a "balloon" payment. If you don't have the cash or don't qualify to refinance your principal, you could lose your home in a court-ordered foreclosure (bank takes ownership).

A Reverse Mortgage

The reverse mortgage program buys your home if you're 62 years of age or older and meet certain criteria.

Positives: You can reside in your home until death. You receive a cash lump-sum, line-of-credit or income stream. Negatives: The mortgage company sells your home upon death, you receive a below-market price for your home to fund your "cash-out," high fees, and complicated contract. Www.FinancilBananaSplit.com for lenders.

Rent-to-Own

Rent-to-own is a structure where part of your rent money is allocated by your landlord towards the purchase of the house. You need to be aware of price relative to comparable homes in the neighborhood, fees, penalties, percentage of your rent allocated to ownership, mortgage interest rate, duration of this process, and proof landlord owns the house (deed/county records).

6. Location

The famous question in real estate is: What are the three most important factors in real estate? Answer: Location, location, location. The "real" in real estate is land ownership. Land is generally the biggest variable in your home's price.

The same house in San Francisco, California, or Wichita, Kansas, will sell for very different prices. Location also determines your home's future value. Besides a luxury location, the next best thing is a house with great future price appreciation due to urban renewal by government or "gentrification" – Older housing being replaced with more expensive housing. Upscale businesses moving in: high-end coffee shops, natural grocery stores. New sidewalks (cobblestone), streetlights.

Check your county clerk's office, local real estate agencies, and www.FinancialBananaSplit.com for the area's recent price appreciation, proposed development, etc.

Location also factors into the "livability" – quality of life – aspects of your house, such as distance, ease, and cost of travel to work, schools, hospitals, transportation, recreation, shopping, places of worship, air quality, noise, etc.

A must do for anyone considering buying a home is to take a walk around the neighborhood six blocks in every direction from the house at different times of day and night to get a feel for where you'll be making this big investment of time and money. Would you be comfortable living there? Neighborhood changing for better? Worse? Imagine driving up to your house every day.

7. Type/Physical Condition

Housing type: Decide which type of dwelling design best fits your current and anticipated future needs, including room for an expanding or extended family.

Elements include:

- Overall square footage
- Number of bedrooms and bathrooms, as well as number of levels and number of stairs to climb.
- Is there a basement/attic/garage? How big is the yard, if any? A larger yard equals higher taxes and maintenance.
- Physical condition: Before you buy, it's advisable to hire a professional home inspector and obtain, in writing, a report detailing the home's total physical condition. Structural, mold, or other damage could cost tens of thousands of dollars to repair.
- Is the house connected to the town sewer and water, or does it have its own well and septic system? What is the condition of the well and septic system? Repairs needed?
- Ask your inspector for cost estimates of planned remodeling.

"Sweat equity" is when you do improvements to the house yourself to save money without hiring professionals. Be realistic about your available time and skill level.

Check with your town if permits are required for electrical, plumbing, or other renovations and applicable zoning regs.

8. Intention and Timing

Intention: Buying a home is a serious commitment. What is your intention for this purchase? Long-term living? Investment? Rental property? Work space?

A basic rule: Don't buy a home as a residence (as opposed to an investment) unless you'll live there at least five years.

Why? Every time you move you pay moving, furniture, mortgage costs, decorating, landscaping, renovations, etc. And you need time for it all. If you're buying a home to "flip" for profit or investment, go to www.FinancialBananaSplit.com for additional resources. All the basic rules of home buying apply to house flipping: comparative pricing, timing, location, cost to renovate.

Timing: Major economic cycles (bad > good > bad) occur about every 12 years. Be aware of where we are in the economic cycle to avoid buying in a housing "bubble" – paying too much for a house because of temporary unrealistic or unsupportable market conditions. "Buy low/sell high" = smartest path to wealth.

Clues? Mortgages given to anyone even with poor credit and no down payment requirements. Housing bubbles also include not enough houses for sale to meet buyer demand. This causes bidding wars for houses above asking price.

If houses in the neighborhood you're considering have risen in price 50% or more over the past five years, talk to homeowners to determine if there is any realistic reason for this dramatic price increase. If there isn't and a crash seems inevitable, be smart and wait. Remember the classic rule: Buy low, sell high.

Paying way too much for housing due to market conditions, unanticipated costly repairs, or any other reason can quickly turn your American Dream into your American Nightmare. Www.FinancialBananaSplit.com for housing market information.

Ingredient Two - Conclusion

Home Ownership gives you the right to say: "There's no place like my home." Work towards owning a home of your own, smartly, by understanding and applying the information presented in this Ingredient.

Ingredient Two: Major Points

1. Home ownership – mortgage free – is a big part of the American Dream.
2. Real estate rises in value over time=wealth creation without another job.
3. Real estate ownership can be an asset to borrow from or an additional income stream as rental income.
4. A mortgage is the type of loan used to buy real estate.
5. The "Step-up" financial pathway to home ownership: Saving to buy a share in a collaboratively owned house > Living in this house > Selling your share for a profit > Using your profit as a down-payment to buy your own home.
6. Home buying basics to understand: Legal rights and obligations – investment benefits – what can you afford: total monthly costs – risks – best mortgage (30 year fixed) – location for value increase – physical condition of property – timing (buy low/sell high) – intention: residence or investment.
7. Monthly Payment of $100,000 30 year fixed-rate mortgage

Interest Rate %	Monthly Payment*
4%	$477.00
5%	$537.00
6%	$600.00
7%	$665.00

* Principal + Interest only. Excludes property taxes, insurance, bank fees and PMI (Pvt. Mtg. Ins. if >20% down payment).

3

Ingredient Three: Loans, Credit, and Debt

Loans, credit, and debt are the ice cream in the banana split. Ways to use money are as numerous as ice cream flavors.

"Beware of little expenses, a small leak will sink a great ship."

(Benjamin Franklin, American statesman, 18th century)

If your credit charges are never fully paid off, they can grow into unmanageable, life-wrecking debt as interest and penalties accumulate.

Avoid this scenario. Use loans, credit, and debt to your financial advantage by understanding what they are, how they work, and how to best manage them. Student loans are a huge issue to many. I explain how to pay off much of this debt using the equity in your home later in the book.

Loan Basics - Definitions

One of the best ways to keep debt under control is to understand how your loan works. This includes credit card debt and how much it actually costs to repay the money you've borrowed.

Definitions of loan terms and documents are explained below:

Credit: Amount of money you're qualified to borrow and that requires repayment.

Debt: Amount of money you've borrowed and requires repayment. Credit turns into debt as soon as it's used.

Creditor: A lender you owe money to such as a bank, credit card company, etc.

Principal: Amount borrowed equal to the purchase price of the item bought.

Interest: Amounts paid by you to the lender for the use of their money, usually expressed as a percentage (%) of the principal (amount borrowed).

Installment Loan: Payments due monthly, etc. (Mtg/auto).

Lender uses one of two methods for interest expense:

1. **Simple interest:** Interest charged only on a loan's outstanding principal balance.
2. **Compound interest:** Interest charged on a loan's outstanding principal balance plus interest charged on the loan's outstanding interest. Compounding can be daily/ monthly/quarterly/ annually. The loan states the frequency.

Compound interest is more expensive than simple interest.

The cost difference between simple and compound interest loans is illustrated as follows:

Example: Loan amount: $30,000/stated interest rate: 6%/ loan duration: 20 years. Simple interest loan – Total interest cost: $21,583 Compound interest loan – Total interest cost: $28,002.

The compound interest loan costs $6,419 more over the life of the loan than the simple interest loan even though both loans have the same stated interest rate and duration.

The "stated" interest rate is the pure interest rate. It doesn't factor in fees, charges or compound interest.

Total interest costs must legally be disclosed on the Truth in Lending Statement (see below).

- **APR** (annual percentage rate): All costs of a loan, including fees, compound interest expenses, and other charges, are converted into a simple interest rate known as the APR. This makes it easier to compare the true costs of various loans. In the example above, the two loans were both offered at the stated interest rate of 6%, but because of the compounding feature in the second loan, its APR would have been shown as 8% on a Truth In Lending Statement.
- **Loan Disclosure Statement:** A lender must disclose all costs and features of a loan on a Loan Disclosure Statement, per federal law. It details loan amount, interest rate – including APR – loan duration, frequency and amount of payments, interest calculation – simple or compound – total interest cost over the life of the loan, fees, costs, and penalties, and how they're triggered. Read, understand, and sign only if you can make all payments. Defaulting on a loan can severely damage your credit. Damaged credit prevents you from obtaining loans, credit cards, a mortgage, renting an apartment, even employment. FinancialBananaSplit.com for Loan Disclosure Statement sample.
- **Secured Debt:** This is when property is pledged as "collateral" (security) to obtain a loan. If you fail to repay the loan, the lender can repossess the collateral. This is usually associated with a mortgage (house loan) or car loan, both of which are assets (things of value).

- **Unsecured Debt:** This is when no property is pledged to obtain a loan. If you fail to repay the loan, the lender can sue you, causing bankruptcy. This is common with credit card debt. A credit card is actually a debt card: It loans you money with interest. The credit used turns into your debt.

Credit

Your credit in the financial world is your reputation, your trustworthiness. It's affected, good and bad, by your actions or damaged by the actions of others, most commonly identity theft.

Let's look at each of these in more detail:

Your Actions

Positive actions affecting your credit:

- Paying bills on time, avoiding late charges and penalties.
- Not using more than 30% of the credit limit on any credit card routinely.
- Using a debit card instead of a credit card for purchases. This keeps your average monthly credit balance low.

Negative actions affecting your credit:

- Not paying bills on time. Incurring late charges and penalties.
- Failure to repay a loan (defaulting).
- Declaring bankruptcy in court.
- Routinely using more than 30% of the credit limit on any credit card.

You need to balance cash back and points against how it might lower your credit score.

True Story - Credit Card

Shortly before I started research for this book, I asked my credit card issuer if they would increase my credit limit. They denied my request because my FICO score was in the low 600s. I couldn't believe it!!

I thought that because I had investments with the same bank that issued my credit card, I wouldn't be denied. I was wrong. Your credit is a separate issue from your overall worth.

After learning the same information presented to you in this book, I took the following steps to raise my FICO score:

- I used my debit card for purchases instead of my credit card.
- I requested my credit records from the three credit bureaus and found an old loan that I was being billed for monthly that I had forgotten about. It wasn't huge, so I paid it off in full.
- There was a recurring charge on my monthly credit card statement for a service I no longer used. I cancelled it.

After taking these three simple steps, my FICO score improved to 823, which is in the "excellent" credit range. Several months later when I applied for my business credit card, the bank granted me double the standard credit limit due in part to my high personal credit score. **I realized I didn't need more credit. I needed to be smarter with the credit I already had.**

Identity Theft

Your financial identity can be attacked and stolen by criminals who use your credit to make unauthorized purchases. This is damaging to your credit and life. Take these steps to monitor, prevent, and repair identity theft:

- Never give your social security number to anyone on the internet or to anyone else unless they can be verified and trusted and their use of your social security number is limited to a specific purpose, in writing.
- Shred all documents with personal financial information before you discard them.
- Don't open or click on internet links or files unless you trust the source.
- Federal law permits you to review your credit reports for free from each of the three credit reporting agencies, Experian, Equifax, and Transunion, once per year.

Use these services to verify the amounts and current status (amounts outstanding, payment due date, etc.) for all debts, including credit cards, car loans, mortgages, etc.

Free credit check sites and links to credit monitoring services which help you avoid being a victim of credit fraud can be found at FinancialBananaSplit.com and Annualcreditreport.com

If you spot problems, take steps to resolve them immediately. Contact the credit card company or other debt issuer, your bank, etc. Address the problem with relevant documents (see below):

If your identity has been stolen, follow these steps:

1. Place a fraud alert on your credit by calling: (800) 685-1111. This prevents any more charges to your credit card.
2. File a police report at your local police station.
3. Create an identity theft report: www.consumer.ftc.gov/topics/repairingidentity-theft.com.
4. Contact the fraud departments of all affected businesses, credit cards and banks using the above reports. Ask your bank to issue a Stop Payment if you paid by check (fee?).

Your Credit Score: FICO

Your credit rating is based on your "FICO" score, a number from 300 to 850. As a direct result of your FICO score your cost to finance (borrow money) can vary greatly.

Example: A $20,000 car loan for 48 months using different credit scores and their costs is illustrated below:

FICO Score	Credit Rating	Interest Rate	Monthly Payment	Interest Expense	Total Cost
720–850	Excellent	3%	$442.69	$1248.95	$21,248.95
690–719	Great	4%	$451.56	$1675.89	$21,675.89
670–689	Very Good	5%	$460.59	$2108.17	$22,108.12
650–669	Good	7%	$478.92	$2988.39	$22,988.12
630–649	Fair	10%	$507.25	$4348.08	$24,348.08
610–629	Poor	12%	$526.68	$5280.48	$25,280.48
580–609	Very Poor	15%	$556.61	$6717.52	$26,717.52

The difference in the cost of the car between an "Excellent" and a "Very Poor" credit rating is over five thousand dollars.

Your credit rating affects interest rates and your ability to qualify for a mortgage or credit cards and might even have a negative impact on your ability to rent housing or secure employment.

Check your credit rating: www.FinancialBananaSplit.com

What Affects Your FICO Score and By How Much

1. Payment history (35%): Missed, late and non-payments.
2. Amounts owed (30%): % of available credit used total / per card >30%.
3. Credit history length (15%): How long you have had credit.

4. Credit mix (10%): Credit cards, mortgage, student loan, car loan, etc.
5. New credit: (10%): # new credit cards, loans, hard credit pulls (A hard credit pull occurs when a potential creditor looks at your entire credit file history).

Establishing Credit

Establishing credit is an important step to take in order to create wealth on your path to economic security. Credit allows you to obtain a mortgage to buy a house, which, when paid off, significantly reduces your living expenses and greatly increases your cash flow.

There are several basic ways to establish credit:

- Put rent, utilities, and internet services in your name. Pay them on time, every month. Late payments will result in a lowered "FICO" score, so keep your payments current.
- Open and maintain a bank checking account. This proves you can manage money and provides documentation to lenders. Find one with no minimum balance fee.
- Obtain a financial institution credit card such as VISA/Discover/MasterCard. You can choose a "standard" credit limit, where the bank will set your limit based on your FICO score and income. Or you can choose a "secured" limit, where you give a deposit to your bank. Your credit limit is this amount.

Controlling Debt

After you've established credit, here's how to stay out of debt:

- Make a monthly budget to be aware of your cash flow. (See Ingredient One: Cash Flow and Banking.)

- Don't charge more than you can pay back every month.
- Treat your credit card like cash: Set up an automatic deduction from your checking account to pay the full amount of all of your credit card charges every month.
- You can use a credit card as little as once every three months for 20 dollars' worth of purchases. This will maintain or even increase your FICO score. It's best to limit its use to emergencies other than the small charge to maintain it. Know your credit card interest rate, penalties, and fees as stated in the credit card agreement, which is a contract.
- Check your bank and credit card statements every month for accuracy, including purchases you didn't make, fees, interest charges, and overcharges.
- Get a debit card from your bank at the same time you get a credit card. With a debit card, money is deducted directly from your checking account the same as a cash payment would be, instead of it going onto your credit card balance. This avoids interest piling up as well as penalties and late fees if you don't fully pay off your credit card(s) totals monthly.
- Pay bills on time to avoid late charges and penalties that will lower your credit rating. Set up automatic monthly bill paying with your bank for recurring charges (rent/utilities/loans, etc.). Make sure you have enough money in your checking account at all times to cover these withdrawals. Ask your bank for their app to check balances using your mobile phone.
- Don't exceed 30% of credit card limits on a regular basis.
- No new debt is the smartest choice for your financial health.

- Cash back, rewards, and free point programs are a tempting incentive to open multiple credit card accounts. Do this only if you can pay off every credit card every month, not use more than 30% of your allowed credit on any card, have plenty of extra cash to pay all debts if you lose your job, and make sure your credit score never drops below 670. Then you might chance having multiple credit cards.

Paying off and staying out of debt is the formula for a successful financial future.

A high debt translates into a lower FICO score and higher borrowing costs. This could mean the difference between qualifying for a mortgage or not and potentially having to file for bankruptcy due to insurmountable debt.

Paying Down Debt Burden - Two Methods

Both methods get you out of debt. The "smart" method might be best if you have a loan with interest exceeding 10%, which is very costly.

Quick Pay-off Method

- Make a list of all debts and their amounts, smallest at the top, largest on the bottom.
- Pay the minimum amount due on all debts.
- Use any extra cash to pay off the smallest debt first.
- When the smallest debt is paid off, do the same for the next debt on your list until it's paid off, and so on, until finished.
- Don't accumulate any new debt until your list is finished. No new debt is the smartest choice for your financial health.

Smart Pay-off Method

- Make a list of all debts with their interest rates, highest interest rate at the top, lowest rate on the bottom.
- Pay the minimum due on all debts.
- Use any extra cash to pay off the debt with the highest interest rate first.
- When that one is paid off, do the same for the next debt on your list until it's paid off, and so on, until finished.
- Don't accumulate any new debt until your list is finished. No new debt is the smartest choice for your financial health.

Debt Consolidation

This technique combines multiple loans into a single, lower-interest loan with lower monthly payments. Collateral is usually required. These loans are typically for a second mortgage or a home equity line of credit. You're putting your house at risk of foreclosure if you default on this loan.

First, contact your creditors to see if they will work with you. Don't accumulate new debt until this loan is paid off. No new debt is the smartest choice for your financial health.

See www.FinancialBananaSplit.com for lender websites.

Credit Counseling

These services offer customized plans to get you out of debt, including budget planning. They work with your creditors to try to extend/forgive/rewrite all or part of your debt to a lower monthly amount you can manage to pay.

You can also call individual creditors first to see if they will work with you. www.FinancialBananaSplit.com for credit counseling services. This list only includes free, non-profit organizations.

Student Loans/Home Equity Loan

I advocate home ownership because "free cash" (due to your home increasing in value) can ease debt burden as follows:

- The average student loan balance is $30,000.
- The average interest rate on this debt is 6.8%.
- The current interest rate on a home equity loan is 4.75% – much less than the student loan rate.

If your home is worth more today than when you purchased it, that value difference can be used as loan collateral to obtain a home equity loan – a second mortgage on your home. Note: Defaulting can cause home loss due to foreclosure.

If you use home equity proceeds to pay off student debt, you'll be able to:

1. Pay back the home equity loan in less time because the same amount of money pays more debt due to its lower interest rate.
2. Pay back the home equity loan for much less interest expense than the student loan due to its lower interest rate.

Example: Student loan $30,000/interest rate 6.8% for 20 years. Monthly payment $229. Total interest expense = $24,960. Home equity loan $30,000/interest rate 4.75% for 20 years. Monthly payment $192. Total interest expense = $16,134.

The difference in interest costs of $8,826 between these two types of loans is huge! Total payback amounts: student loan $54,960 vs. home equity loan $46,134. Why pay more for the same thing?

It pays to get and stay on the path to the American Dream. In other words: Get ye into home ownership.

If you can't take advantage of a home equity loan to pay off your student loan, consider other options and ask your lender about forbearance and deferment. These options allow you to postpone loan payments: deferment, without accruing interest, and forbearance, while still accruing interest. A job during college lets you pay off student debt as it happens.

Paying For College: Student Loans, Grants, Etc.

There are many ways to pay for college: A Job/ Military Service / Student Loans and Grants / Work-Study Programs, etc. And advice is available. The student aid office of the college you are considering should be a valuable resource. The federal government administers the largest student loan program: Federal Student Aid. Contact: www.studentaid.gov/ > Considering school > or Contact Us or Help Center. Tele# 1(800) 433 – 3243 / Live chat and e-mail available on their website.

True Story - College Job

My parents and grandparents were able to pay my college tuition but any extra spending money I had to earn myself.

I got a job as the delivery person for a local florist near my school in Washington, DC. It was used by many prominent politicians as well as wealthy people in the Capital area.

As I was the regular delivery person, I had the opportunity to see inside many mansions, including one where former Secretary of State Henry Kissinger would be a dinner guest. I also delivered flowers to the infamous Watergate Hotel where Republican operatives, allegedly with the knowledge of then President Nixon, broke into the Democrats' campaign headquarters to steal information (two years before my time).

This incident was depicted in a famous movie when the main character sees flashlights moving inside a Washington DC hotel room and calls the front desk to investigate.

My best delivery memories were when I'd walk into a hospital waiting room with a huge bouquet of flowers (destined for a VIP patient), and everybody (patients, staff, visitors) would light up like Fourth of July fireworks.

Moral of the story: Strive for financial independence, set a pattern for yourself now. You never know what positive adventures and memories await.

Debt Burden: Impossible

Bad things happen when you're unable to pay debts. It can make your life a horror show when you're unable to obtain credit cards, car loans, student loans, or buy a house. You can also be turned down for jobs, apartment rentals, utilities, cell phones, and even dates. Yes, a date might ask to see your credit score on your phone – before committing to a more serious relationship.

Bad credit requiring legal action tells the world you're a loser. Don't be a loser. Learn these techniques to avoid Loserville. To keep bad things from happening, it's all about being aware of your cash flow: inflow versus outflow. This means not spending more than you take in each month.

What are the biggest expenses in your life?

Student loans? Technology? Debt? Clothes? Entertainment? Want another tattoo? Get it the first day you move into your own home. That's one even your parents won't object to. You are the parent? Want to retire but can't yet? Both of you need to:

1. Complete your monthly budget on page 17.

2. Follow this book's path to the American Dream.

Financial Bad Stuff to Avoid

Collection Agencies

Collection agencies are hired by creditors to collect debt. They report their progress/status to the credit bureaus. Non-payment can lead to a lowering of your FICO score and a bad credit rating.

If you're contacted by a collection agency, take these steps:

- Ask the collection agency to send written proof of all debts.
- Write them a "cease and desist" letter and send it by certified mail. This ends the collection agency's right to keep contacting you for the same debt, although they can continue other actions: FICO reporting, legal action, paycheck garnishment, etc.

(See sample letter: www.FinancialBananaSplit.com). Verify your debts by contacting your creditors and making arrangements to pay them off as soon as possible.

Bankruptcy

Bankruptcy is a legal process filed by you or on your behalf in court to give you protection from creditors while you plan and settle (or have dismissed) unpayable debts.

The two most common forms of personal bankruptcy are:

- Chapter 7 Bankruptcy: Liquidation of assets to permanently discharge debts. Assets to be sold: House, car, boat, jewelry, savings, etc. Debts that cannot be discharged: Taxes, mortgages, student loans, alimony, child support, and medical bills. Once a debt is discharged through Chapter 7, it is gone forever.

- Chapter 13 Bankruptcy: Reorganization and repayment. You are required to make court-ordered payments to creditors. Selling of assets is optional. The court decides payment schedule.

Bankruptcy makes it difficult to re-establish full credit for seven years. To fix, read Establishing Credit, on page 52. You can file for bankruptcy using an attorney, a non-attorney bankruptcy petition preparer, or bankruptcy software. These services have different costs and levels of accuracy. Contact the county clerk, state BAR (lawyers) association, or www.FinancialBananaSplit.com for resources.

Foreclosure

Foreclosure is a legal process where you lose your home due to an inability to pay your mortgage.

- You are court ordered to vacate your home (sheriff notified).
- All credit cards are cancelled.
- You can re-establish your credit by following Establishing Credit, above. Mortgages take seven years to requalify.

Ingredient Three - Conclusion

You can keep on the path to the American Dream if you understand cash flow, follow your budget, and use loans/credit/debt to strengthen, not weaken, your financial life.

Ingredient Three: Major Points

1. Unpaid credit charges are unsustainable: interest charges, penalties, fees.
2. Loans, credit and debt: Understand how they work and how

to manage to use them to your financial advantage: mortgage for house, better credit = lower loan costs.

3. Definitions: Credit=amount you qualify to borrow/Debt= requires repayment/Creditor=who you owe/Principal=amount initially borrowed/Interest=cost added to principal/APR=annual percentage rate for loan/ Secured debt requires collateral (asset) you can lose/Compound interest is more costly than simple interest/Loan Disclosure Statement =legally required by lender.
4. FICO score= credit rating: 300>850 = poor to excellent. 760+ is the goal.
5. Federal law permits you to review your credit reports for free from each credit reporting agency: Experian, Equifax, and Transunion, once per year: www.Annualcreditreport.com
6. Report credit errors/theft immediately to credit card company or bank.
7. Establishing credit: Utilities, rent, bank account in your name. Pay on-time.
8. Successful financial future = Pay on-time/use 30% max. of credit limit.
9. Debt payoff methods: Pay minimum amounts due every month. Quick=smallest debt 1st/Smart=highest interest debt 1st/Credit counseling helps you organize debt repayment-maybe reduce/Debt Consolidation =small debts rolled into one larger debt: lower monthly payment.
10. Collection Agencies/Bankruptcy-2 types/Foreclosure

4

Ingredient Four: Avoiding Financial Landmines

Avoiding Financial Landmines are the banana split toppings, covering other Ingredients and affecting their overall flavor.

Certain basics need to be included in your financial planning to avoid paying unforeseen legal costs, fees, penalties, etc.

Protect your money by following the guidelines outlined below for income taxes, contracts, insurance, dealing with documents, and estate planning.

Income Taxes

"In this world nothing is certain except death and taxes."

(Benjamin Franklin, American statesman, 1789)

Income taxes are the only taxes you've got to actively compute every year. Once done, you'll pay either less in taxes or receive a bigger refund for taxes paid than if you hadn't made the effort. Ignoring this can result in property seizure, bankruptcy, bad credit, and even prison for fraud.

You can minimize your taxes and stay out of trouble by following these income tax basics.

Filing Your Annual Federal Income Tax Return

All individual/married taxpayers file their Federal Income Taxes using Form 1040. However, there are additional forms and documents necessary to be filed with the 1040 to accurately reflect your total taxable income and allowable deductions (as applicable)

Common Forms Used to File Your 1040 Tax Return (as needed)

Identification

1. Name/address/SS#.
2. Valid Govt. Issued I.D.
3. Prior Year 1040-if filed.

Proof of Income Documents

1. W-2: Job Wages & Salary.
2. 1099 NT: Interest Income.
3. 1099 DIV: Dividend Income.
4. 1099 MISC: Self-Employment Income.
5. 1099 G: Government payments to you.
6. SSA-1099: Social Security benefits.
7. Schedule K-1: Partnership Income/Loss.

Proof of Deduction Documents

1. 1098: Mortgage Interest.
2. 1098-E: Student Loan Interest.
3. 1098-T: Tuition.
4. 1095: Heath Care Coverage.
5. Receipts for Charitable Donations.
6. Contributions to Retirement Plans-not IRA.
7. Child Care Expenses w/ SS# of caregiver.
8. Self-Employment Income/ Expenses-home office, health insurance, supplies, expenses.
9. Moving Expenses to a New Job.

Example Illustrating Tax Savings Having and Using Tax Deductions

No Deductions = Higher Tax Liability	**Deductions = Lower Tax Liability**
Gross Income: $55,000	Gross Income: $55,000
Less Standard Deduction: $12,950	Less Standard Deduction: $12,950
Adjusted Gross Income: $42,250	Less Pension Contribution: $5,000
Rate for this tax bracket: 22%	Less Student Loan Interest: $3,000
Total 1040 Tax Liability: **$9,295**	Adjusted Gross Income: $35,950
	Rate for this tax bracket: 12%
	Total 1040 Tax Liability: **$4,314**

Above, having and using tax deductions saved $4,981 in taxes owed. This almost equaled the entire $5,000 pension contribution! Deductions are calculated and inputted onto the appropriate IRS schedule and filed with your 1040. Most-used 1040 schedules include: Schedule A: Itemized deductions / B: Interest and ordinary dividends/ C: Profit/loss from business / D: Capital gains and losses / R: Credit for elderly or disabled, etc.

You can file your 1040 – along with your state income tax return if required in your state-1. By mail (slowest processing) 2. E-file on-line 3. Use tax preparation software. Do the work yourself or pay a tax preparer. Refunds are slowest by mail, faster by e-filing. Free govt. assistance: irs.gov > Help > File a Return / Tele# (800) 829 – 1040.

See the Maintaining Documents section below for which documents to keep for what time period to support tax filing. Federal govt. can audit you for three years after filing a tax return - forever if fraud.

Filing your Annual State Income Tax Return

Most states charge income tax on resident's wages/salary/investment/ interest income. In these states residents must file a state income tax return with the state and one with their Federal Income Tax Return (1040). Rates vary from 1% (GA) > 13.3% (CA). States without a state income tax include: AK/FL/NV/NH/SD/TN/TX/WA/WY. Contact or on-line your state's tax department for the proper forms and instructions. Some cities (NYC) and counties also impose an income tax on their residents. Contact or on-line your city/county to verify taxable status of your earned / investment income.

Income Tax - Basic Definitions

Know these basic definitions to understand income taxes:

Income Tax – A tax on your earnings collected by a government (federal/state/city). Example: Federal income tax is collected annually by the IRS (Internal Revenue Service).

Income Tax Rate – A percentage of income used to calculate income taxes owed.

Taxable Earnings – Income received from jobs, tips, investments, rents, gifts, etc. (certain exclusions apply).

Taxpayer – A resident of the United States earning over $10,300 annually (subject to change).

Income Tax Deduction – Amount deducted from income to reduce taxes owed. Examples: Pension contribution, student loan interest, property taxes, mortgage interest, etc.

Income Tax Credit – Amount deducted from your total tax liability, which reduces taxes owed. Examples: Earned income tax credit, solar panels for house, Child and Dependent Care, Lifetime Learning, American Opportunity (college), etc.

Personal Tax Exemption – An amount allowed by the IRS, deducted from income, that reduces taxes owed. Example: The Standard Exemption for single taxpayers is $12,000.

Tax Filing – Submitting your tax return to the government. Example: 1040EZ/1040A/1040.

Filing Deadline – Date income tax return due. Example: Federal returns are due every April 15th for individuals.

Tax Year: Year for which taxes are due. Example: Calendar year for individuals is Jan.–Dec.

Income Documentation: Documents showing earnings during the tax year. Examples: W-2 wage statement, 1099 bank interest, and investment income.

Deduction Documentation: Documents showing qualified (as allowed by the IRS or state of residence) expense or loss. Examples: Medical bills, loan interest documents, charity receipts, pension contributions, state income taxes paid, etc.

Your Paycheck: Forms/Earnings /Withholding/Deductions

Form W-4: An employer-issued document completed by the employee. Employer uses it to compute and deduct taxes from your paycheck. More deductions =less taxes=more take-home pay. Ex: Married or single/ # of dependents/ income from other jobs, etc.

Form W-2: Issued by employer yearly and reported to the IRS. It shows total wages and taxes deducted from your paycheck. You file it with your Income Tax Return.

Pay Stub: A paycheck document noting: Gross/Net Earnings, Pay Rate/Period, Deductions and I.D. Info. (See sample).

Gross Pay: Total amount earned for a paycheck period.

Net Pay: Gross pay minus all withholding and deductions.

Form **W-4**

Department of the Treasury
Internal Revenue Service

Employee's Withholding Certificate

▶ Complete Form W-4 so that your employer can withhold the correct federal income tax from your pay.
▶ Give Form W-4 to your employer.
▶ Your withholding is subject to review by the IRS.

OMB No. 1545-0074

2022

Step 1: Enter Personal Information	(a) First name and middle initial	Last name	(b) Social security number
	Address		▶ **Does your name match the name on your social security card?** If not, to ensure you get credit for your earnings, contact SSA at 800-772-1213 or go to *www.ssa.gov*.
	City or town, state, and ZIP code		
	(c) ☐ **Single** or **Married filing separately** ☐ **Married filing jointly** or **Qualifying widow(er)** ☐ **Head of household** (Check only if you're unmarried and pay more than half the costs of keeping up a home for yourself and a qualifying individual.)		

Complete Steps 2–4 ONLY if they apply to you; otherwise, skip to Step 5. See page 2 for more information on each step, who can claim exemption from withholding, when to use the estimator at *www.irs.gov/W4App*, and privacy.

Step 2: Multiple Jobs or Spouse Works

Complete this step if you (1) hold more than one job at a time, or (2) are married filing jointly and your spouse also works. The correct amount of withholding depends on income earned from all of these jobs.

Do **only one** of the following.

(a) Use the estimator at *www.irs.gov/W4App* for most accurate withholding for this step (and Steps 3–4); **or**

(b) Use the Multiple Jobs Worksheet on page 3 and enter the result in Step 4(c) below for roughly accurate withholding; **or**

(c) If there are only two jobs total, you may check this box. Do the same on Form W-4 for the other job. This option is accurate for jobs with similar pay; otherwise, more tax than necessary may be withheld . . . ▶ ☐

TIP: To be accurate, submit a 2022 Form W-4 for all other jobs. If you (or your spouse) have self-employment income, including as an independent contractor, use the estimator.

Complete Steps 3–4(b) on Form W-4 for only ONE of these jobs. Leave those steps blank for the other jobs. (Your withholding will be most accurate if you complete Steps 3–4(b) on the Form W-4 for the highest paying job.)

Step 3: Claim Dependents

If your total income will be $200,000 or less ($400,000 or less if married filing jointly):

Multiply the number of qualifying children under age 17 by $2,000 ▶ $ ________

Multiply the number of other dependents by $500 . . . . ▶ $ ________

Add the amounts above and enter the total here . . . . | **3** | $

Step 4 (optional): Other Adjustments

(a) Other income (not from jobs). If you want tax withheld for other income you expect this year that won't have withholding, enter the amount of other income here. This may include interest, dividends, and retirement income . . . . | **4(a)** | $

(b) Deductions. If you expect to claim deductions other than the standard deduction and want to reduce your withholding, use the Deductions Worksheet on page 3 and enter the result here . . . . | **4(b)** | $

(c) Extra withholding. Enter any additional tax you want withheld each **pay period** . . | **4(c)** | $

Step 5: Sign Here

Under penalties of perjury, I declare that this certificate, to the best of my knowledge and belief, is true, correct, and complete.

▶ **Employee's signature** (This form is not valid unless you sign it.) ▶ **Date**

Employers Only	Employer's name and address	First date of employment	Employer identification number (EIN)

For Privacy Act and Paperwork Reduction Act Notice, see page 3. Cat. No. 10220Q Form **W-4** (2022)

22222	VOID ☐	a Employee's social security number	For Official Use Only ▶ OMB No. 1545-0008
b Employer identification number (EIN)		1 Wages, tips, other compensation	2 Federal income tax withheld
c Employer's name, address, and ZIP code		3 Social security wages	4 Social security tax withheld
		5 Medicare wages and tips	6 Medicare tax withheld
		7 Social security tips	8 Allocated tips
d Control number		9	10 Dependent care benefits
e Employee's first name and initial	Last name / Suff.	11 Nonqualified plans	12a See instructions for box 12
		13 Statutory employee ☐ Retirement plan ☐ Third-party sick pay ☐	12b
		14 Other	12c
f Employee's address and ZIP code			12d

15 State	Employer's state ID number	16 State wages, tips, etc.	17 State income tax	18 Local wages, tips, etc.	19 Local income tax	20 Locality name

Form **W-2** **Wage and Tax Statement** 2022

Department of the Treasury—Internal Revenue Service

For Privacy Act and Paperwork Reduction Act Notice, see the separate instructions.

Cat. No. 10134D

Copy A—For Social Security Administration. Send this entire page with Form W-3 to the Social Security Administration; photocopies are **not** acceptable.

Do Not Cut, Fold, or Staple Forms on This Page

Pay stub (hourly)

SMITH AND COMPANY, INC.
123 West Street Smalltown, CA 98765

EMPLOYEE	SOCIAL SECURITY NO.	PAY RATE	PAY PERIOD
Johnson, Bob	XXX-XX-6789	18.00 regular 27.00 overtime	1/7/XX to 1/13/XX

EARNINGS	HOURS	AMOUNT
Regular	40.00	720.00
Overtime	2.00	54.00

GROSS EARNINGS:	774.00
TOTAL DEDUCTED:	213.29
NET EARNINGS:	560.71

DEDUCTIONS	AMOUNT
Federal W/H	60.45
FICA	47.99
Medicare	11.22
CA State W/H	10.04
CA State DI	6.19
401k	77.40

SICK LEAVE:
24.00 **HOURS AVAILABLE**

Example itemized wage statement (pay stub) for a worker paid hourly.

May 2018

Form **1040** Department of the Treasury—Internal Revenue Service (99)
U.S. Individual Income Tax Return **2021** OMB No. 1545-0074 IRS Use Only—Do not write or staple in this space.

Filing Status Check only one box. ☐ Single ☐ Married filing jointly ☐ Married filing separately (MFS) ☐ Head of household (HOH) ☐ Qualifying widow(er) (QW)
If you checked the MFS box, enter the name of your spouse. If you checked the HOH or QW box, enter the child's name if the qualifying person is a child but not your dependent ▶

Your first name and middle initial	Last name	**Your social security number**
If joint return, spouse's first name and middle initial	Last name	**Spouse's social security number**

Home address (number and street). If you have a P.O. box, see instructions.		Apt. no.	**Presidential Election Campaign** Check here if you, or your spouse if filing jointly, want $3 to go to this fund. Checking a box below will not change your tax or refund. ☐ You ☐ Spouse
City, town, or post office. If you have a foreign address, also complete spaces below.	State	ZIP code	
Foreign country name	Foreign province/state/county	Foreign postal code	

At any time during 2021, did you receive, sell, exchange, or otherwise dispose of any financial interest in any virtual currency? ☐ Yes ☐ No

Standard Deduction **Someone can claim:** ☐ You as a dependent ☐ Your spouse as a dependent
☐ Spouse itemizes on a separate return or you were a dual-status alien

Age/Blindness **You:** ☐ Were born before January 2, 1957 ☐ Are blind **Spouse:** ☐ Was born before January 2, 1957 ☐ Is blind

Dependents (see instructions):
If more than four dependents, see instructions and check here ▶ ☐

(1) First name Last name	(2) Social security number	(3) Relationship to you	(4) ✔ if qualifies for (see instructions): Child tax credit	Credit for other dependents
			☐	☐
			☐	☐
			☐	☐
			☐	☐

Attach Sch. B if required.

1	Wages, salaries, tips, etc. Attach Form(s) W-2			1	
2a	Tax-exempt interest	2a	b Taxable interest	2b	
3a	Qualified dividends	3a	b Ordinary dividends	3b	
4a	IRA distributions	4a	b Taxable amount	4b	
5a	Pensions and annuities	5a	b Taxable amount	5b	
6a	Social security benefits	6a	b Taxable amount	6b	
7	Capital gain or (loss). Attach Schedule D if required. If not required, check here ▶ ☐			7	
8	Other income from Schedule 1, line 10			8	
9	Add lines 1, 2b, 3b, 4b, 5b, 6b, 7, and 8. This is your **total income** ▶			9	
10	Adjustments to income from Schedule 1, line 26			10	
11	Subtract line 10 from line 9. This is your **adjusted gross income** ▶			11	
12a	**Standard deduction or itemized deductions** (from Schedule A)	12a			
b	Charitable contributions if you take the standard deduction (see instructions)	12b			
c	Add lines 12a and 12b			12c	
13	Qualified business income deduction from Form 8995 or Form 8995-A			13	
14	Add lines 12c and 13			14	
15	**Taxable income.** Subtract line 14 from line 11. If zero or less, enter -0-			15	

Standard Deduction for—
- Single or Married filing separately, $12,550
- Married filing jointly or Qualifying widow(er), $25,100
- Head of household, $18,800
- If you checked any box under *Standard Deduction,* see instructions.

For Disclosure, Privacy Act, and Paperwork Reduction Act Notice, see separate instructions. Cat. No. 11320B Form **1040** (2021)

Form 1040 (2021) Page 2

16	**Tax** (see instructions). Check if any from Form(s): 1 ☐ 8814 2 ☐ 4972 3 ☐ ______			16
17	Amount from Schedule 2, line 3			17
18	Add lines 16 and 17			18
19	Nonrefundable child tax credit or credit for other dependents from Schedule 8812			19
20	Amount from Schedule 3, line 8			20
21	Add lines 19 and 20			21
22	Subtract line 21 from line 18. If zero or less, enter -0-			22
23	Other taxes, including self-employment tax, from Schedule 2, line 21			23
24	Add lines 22 and 23. This is your **total tax** ▶			24
25	Federal income tax withheld from:			
a	Form(s) W-2	25a		
b	Form(s) 1099	25b		
c	Other forms (see instructions)	25c		
d	Add lines 25a through 25c			25d
26	2021 estimated tax payments and amount applied from 2020 return			26
27a	Earned income credit (EIC)	27a		
	Check here if you were born after January 1, 1998, and before January 2, 2004, and you satisfy all the other requirements for taxpayers who are at least age 18, to claim the EIC. See instructions ▶ ☐			
b	Nontaxable combat pay election	27b		
c	Prior year (2019) earned income	27c		
28	Refundable child tax credit or additional child tax credit from Schedule 8812	28		
29	American opportunity credit from Form 8863, line 8	29		
30	Recovery rebate credit. See instructions	30		
31	Amount from Schedule 3, line 15	31		
32	Add lines 27a and 28 through 31. These are your **total other payments and refundable credits** ▶			32
33	Add lines 25d, 26, and 32. These are your **total payments** ▶			33

If you have a qualifying child, attach Sch. EIC.

Refund

Direct deposit? See instructions.

34	If line 33 is more than line 24, subtract line 24 from line 33. This is the amount you **overpaid**		34
35a	Amount of line 34 you want **refunded to you.** If Form 8888 is attached, check here ▶ ☐		35a
▶b	Routing number ▶ c Type: ☐ Checking ☐ Savings		
▶d	Account number		
36	Amount of line 34 you want **applied to your 2022 estimated tax** ▶	36	

Amount You Owe

37	**Amount you owe.** Subtract line 33 from line 24. For details on how to pay, see instructions ▶		37
38	Estimated tax penalty (see instructions) ▶	38	

Third Party Designee

Do you want to allow another person to discuss this return with the IRS? See instructions ▶ ☐ **Yes.** Complete below. ☐ **No**

Designee's name ▶ | Phone no. ▶ | Personal identification number (PIN) ▶

Sign Here

Under penalties of perjury, I declare that I have examined this return and accompanying schedules and statements, and to the best of my knowledge and belief, they are true, correct, and complete. Declaration of preparer (other than taxpayer) is based on all information of which preparer has any knowledge.

Joint return? See instructions. Keep a copy for your records.

Your signature	Date	Your occupation	If the IRS sent you an Identity Protection PIN, enter it here (see inst.) ▶
Spouse's signature. If a joint return, **both** must sign.	Date	Spouse's occupation	If the IRS sent your spouse an Identity Protection PIN, enter it here (see inst.) ▶
Phone no.	Email address		

Paid Preparer Use Only

Preparer's name	Preparer's signature	Date	PTIN	Check if: ☐ Self-employed
Firm's name ▶			Phone no.	
Firm's address ▶			Firm's EIN ▶	

Go to *www.irs.gov/Form1040* for instructions and the latest information. Form **1040** (2021)

Withholding: Government deductions: federal + state income taxes/ FICA: Social Security +Medicare/ unemployment + worker's compensation insurance. Your employer is required to match your FICA deduction and credit it to your federal account. You can request a free status report on your federal account at: www.irs.gov.

Deductions: Voluntary and employee benefit type deductions. Some deductions are deductible from your taxable income = lower taxes = more take-home pay. Ex: pension (401K), life insurance, health insurance with high deductible. Disability insurance is not deductible because it is considered income.

Local Tax Considerations (Non-income tax)

There are government taxing authorities at the state and local levels who add tax to various activities to generate revenue to keep governments operational. For citizens (non-business taxes), these taxes often include:

1. **Sales Tax(s):** A state tax levied on most purchases, excluding rent or the purchase of real estate. Clothes, cars, appliances, services, utilities, food, etc.

   The sales tax rate varies by state from 0% (OR,DE,MO,NH) to 7.25% (CA). A local sales tax is often added to the state sales tax by a city or town. Example: Florida: 6% state sales tax + 1.05% local sales tax = 7.05% sales tax total.

2. **Property Tax:** Most counties levy (charge) taxes on the value of a house (assessed or fair market value) to pay for schools, police, fire dept., sanitation collection, etc. The rate varies widely per county. The average = 1%. Example: A house valued at $300,000 dollars for tax purposes with a 1% property tax

rate would pay $3,000 per year in property taxes. You generally receive a tax bill from the county, as a home owner, once per year. It gives a detailed breakdown of all the services supported by your property taxes. A dispute mechanism is available if you believe you've been overcharged. Taxes are generally payable in two installments six months apart.

Contracts

Definition: A contract is an agreement between parties for an exchange of something of value creating mutual obligations enforceable by law.

Contract - Six Required Legal Elements

1. **Offer:** Something must be offered and the requirements / performance/ obligations of each party stated to fulfill the contract.
2. **Acceptance:** The offeree can show their acceptance in writing (signature/date) or verbally if allowed by the Statute of Frauds. Most types of contracts require signing: real estate, sale of goods over $500 dollars, in consideration of marriage and duration over 1 year are the most common examples.
3. **Consideration:** Something of value has to be promised: an asset, action or agreement for non-action, to be exchanged between the parties.
4. **Awareness:** All parties to the contract must be active participants, understand what they are getting involved in and be free to do so.
5. **Capacity:** A person would not have the capacity to enter into a legally binding contract if they are: a) a minor 2) intoxicated 3)

unable to comprehend the contract language 4) are otherwise mentally incapacitated – dementia, etc.

6. **Legality:** A contract for an illegal product or action can't be legally enforced. Example: A contract for murder. Different states allow different things if not prohibited by federal law.

Whether it's titled a contract, lease, loan, agreement, mortgage, promissory note, etc., *if it contains the six legal elements of a contract* **... it's a contract!**

Contracts are legally binding documents. All signors to the contract are obligated to comply with all terms and conditions or pay costs, incur legal fees, or receive a lowered credit rating for non-compliance, etc.

** READ THE ENTIRE CONTRACT BEFORE SIGNING **

Don't sign any contract until you can identify, understand, and agree to all terms and conditions.

What To Look for In a Contract – 10 Points

1. **Payment:** What will you pay, or what will you be paid? Minimum, maximum, weekly, monthly, total, etc.
2. **Non-compliance:** Are there consequences? Penalties, charges, obligations?
3. **Termination:** Automatically ends or renews? Notice given? By whom?
4. **Duration of contract:** Specific time frame or open-ended?
5. **Performance:** What is required specifically of you and the seller (gym, phone company, landlord, car lease) to be done?
6. **Returns:** Items need to be returned when, how, and in what condition? Penalties?

7. **Assignment:** Is the contract "assignable" (transferrable to others) by you or seller? Any additional charges?
8. **Buy option:** Available? When? Price, fees, taxes, other conditions?
9. **Getting the best deal:** Receiving all applicable discounts, rebates, competitor's coupons, trade-ins, etc.?
10. **Insurance:** Who pays for property damage insurance and liability insurance, if required?

How to Review A Contract - Three Steps

1. Start with point 1, above – Payments. Identify all payment related terms and conditions in the contract.
2. Ask the seller to clarify anything you don't understand.
3. Negotiate your best deal or anything you're not comfortable with. If unable to resolve – Do Not Sign The Contract!

True Story - Former Boss

My former boss was an old school bookkeeper who was always being marketed to by young, smart, professional, smooth-talking salespeople.

They presented their sales pitch in a complex manner trying to mask reality, hoping she was too intimidated by a lack of understanding to ask questions and just accept and sign.

One day I was in her office and witnessed a sales pitch. She kept asking questions and couldn't understand the full consequences of buying this particular product (hand soap dispensers).

Instead of being intimidated, feeling stupid, or signing the contract, she simply said, "I can't buy something I don't understand. Come back when you can explain it to me better."

In other words, she wasn't the problem; the salesperson was. If he couldn't explain something in terms that were understandable to her, he was the one who was ignorant. You do the same. If you can't repeat to the salesperson exactly what the product or service is they're selling, don't sign the contract.

Examples: A Contract and Personal Loan Application

THE SIMPLE CONTRACT LAWN COMPANY

This Contract is entered into this _____ day of __________ by and between: ____(COMPANY), and ____(CLIENT).

The term of this agreement shall be for one year beginning on ____________________ and ending on ______________________.

The specific terms of this Contract are as follows:

1. The company shall provide lawn care services on a year-round basis to client at their residential address.
2. Said services shall include once-per-week lawn mowing and brush trimming to the outside area including haul-away of all trimmings and debris per service.
3. Total annual price for this service shall be _________ dollars, payable in equal monthly installments of _________ dollars per month.
4. Additional services as requested by client shall be billed separately.

In consideration of the mutual promises as set forth herein, the Company covenants and agrees that it shall ____________________ ____.

The Client covenants and agrees that it shall ________________ ____.

This contract may not be modified in any manner unless in writing and signed by both parties. This document and any attachments hereto constitute the entire agreement between the Parties.

This Contract shall be binding upon both Parties, their successors, heirs and assigns and shall be enforced under the laws of the State of ________________.

______________________________	______________________________
(Client Signature)	(Company Signature)
______________________________	______________________________
(Printed Name)	(Printed Name)
DATE: ______________________	DATE: ______________________

SIMPLE BANK
PERSONAL LOAN APPLICATION

Each loan application is assessed individually. There is no guarantee of a loan. This loan application is not considered completed until all requested supporting documents are submitted.

NAME OF BORROWER____________________________________

DATE OF BIRTH ____________ Phone # ____________ SS# ________
CURRENT ADDRESS ____________________________________
TIME AT THIS ADDRESS ________ (CIRCLE): OWN RENT MONTHLY RENT $________
IF LESS THAN # YEARS LIST PRIOR ADDRESS(S): ________________

____

EMPLOYMENT STATUS (CIRCLE): EMPLOYED/ SELF-EMPLOYED/ RETIRED/OTHER
NAME OF EMPLOYER ____________________________________
ADDRESS OF EMPLOYER ____________________________________
OCCUPATION _____ YEARS EMPLOYED ___ IF LESS THAN 3 YEARS LIST OTHER EMPLOYMENT OR INCOME SOURCE: ____________

____

SUPPORTING DOCUMENTATION CHECKLIST

1. IDENTIFICATION: DRIVER'S LICENSE, PASSPORT, OTHER GOVERNMENT DOC.
2. PROOF OF INCOME AND CREDIT WORTHINESS:
   a) 3 MOST RECENT WAGE STATEMENTS (PAY STUBS) FROM CURRENT JOB(S).
   b) BANK STATEMENTS: LAST # MONTHS FOR EVERY ACCOUNT.
   c) CREDIT CARD(S): MOST RECENT STATEMENT FOR EVERY CREDIT CARD.
3. ARE YOU A CO-SIGNOR OR GUARANTOR ON ANY DEBT OR LOAN? ________
   IF YES: AMOUNT $_________ DURATION _________ DEBTOR _________

4. PROOF OF ANY PRIOR LOAN REPAYMENT(S), IF APPLICABLE.

WHEN OUR BANK ACCEPTS YOUR LOAN APPLICATION, OUR UNDERWRITING DEPARTMENT WILL REVIEW ALL DOCUMENTS, CONDUCT A CREDIT CHECK AND TAKE ALL STEPS NECESSARYTO ASCERTAIN YOUR LOAN QUALIFICATIONS. IF YOU ARE

APPROVED, YOU WILL BE GIVEN A LOAN CONTRACT STATING THE LOAN AMOUNT, INTEREST RATE AND ALL OTHER REPAYMENT TERMS AND CONDITIONS FOR REVIEW AND SIGNATURE. IF APPROVED, LOAN IS GRANTED.

IT IS A CRIME TO GIVE FALSE INFORMATION OR DOCUMENTS IN ORDER TO OBTAIN A LOAN, PUNISHIBLE UNDER STATE CRIMINAL CODE SL467BH9.

I HAVE READ, UNDERSTOOD AND AGREE TO ALL OF THE ABOVE. I GRANT THE BANK PERMISSION TO CONDUCT CREDIT SEARCHES AND ALL ELSE AS NECESSARY TO DETERMINE MY LOAN QUALIFICATIONS.

________________________ ________________________

(SIGNATURE OF APPLICANT) (DATE)

____

(PRINT NAME)

Insurance

The purpose of insurance is to protect you and your loved ones financially from damage and losses to property and life, including accidents caused by you. Liability = bodily injury.

A "deductible" is the amount you pay for losses before the insurance company pays. The higher the deductible, the lower your insurance policy "premium" (cost to buy) should be.

How much insurance coverage do you need? A general rule is to buy the amount of insurance that protects your assets (savings/car/house, etc.) from having to be sold to pay claims, which could leave you broke and possibly filing for bankruptcy.

Different insurance types and coverages are explained below:

- **Renter's Insurance** – Coverage needs to pay for injury to you and others (liability) while in your apartment and replacement of belongings (property) in case they are destroyed or stolen. Example: You fail to purchase renter's insurance for your apartment. A friend visits. She slips and falls on your wet kitchen floor, injuring herself, requiring hospitalization with $19,000 in medical bills. She sues you and your landlord. You lose in court and are ordered to pay. Now you have to empty your savings account of its entire $5,000 and sell your car to get an additional $14,000 to comply with the court order. Inexpensive renter's insurance ($150 per year?) would have covered this, and the insurance company would have defended you in court.

- **Auto Insurance** – Liability coverage pays for injury to others. Medical and Personal Injury Protection coverage pays your medical expenses. Collision and Comprehensive coverage pays for vehicle damage.
- **Healthcare Insurance** – Coverage needs to pay for all medical costs and continuing care for all persons included in the policy. It's expensive. It's a huge benefit if paid by your employer.
- **Disability Insurance:** Pays part/all of salary if unable to work.
- **Long-Term Care Insurance**: Pays expensive elder nursing home care.
- **House Insurance** – Coverage needs to pay for fire damage, damage caused by acts of nature (hurricanes, fire, flood, etc.), and injury to persons in your house or on your property (liability insurance) – the same injury consequences as renter's insurance, above.
- **Life Insurance** – Pays upon the death of the insured. Coverage should have a death benefit big enough to support loved ones who depend on your financial support to pay mortgage costs, health bills, education, and living costs for the time needed.

There are two main types of life insurance: term and whole life.

Term life insurance: Low annual cost. No coverage if you stop paying. Coverage is for a specified number of years. Renewal is necessary after the term ends, at which point you'll need to requalify, probably at a higher rate because you're older.

Whole life insurance: Once you buy a policy renewal is not necessary unless you fail to pay premiums before the policy self-funds (the policy earns annual dividends equal to or greater than the annual premium). Coverage lasts until your death regardless of your health status. You can borrow the "cash value" in your policy, which increases over time as premiums are paid. The policy can increase in value over time, similar to an investment.

I believe you should, as a minimum, purchase an inexpensive term life insurance policy on your life if there is anyone who depends or will depend on you financially (wife/children/ partner). This will replace your lost income for them.

Or, if no one depends on you financially but you want to throw an unforgettable New Orleans/Mardi Gras-style funeral party when you die, it'll only happen if you leave enough money for that event plus a big tip for the person who's to arrange it all.

Whole life insurance is wise to purchase when you have extra money – an automatic deduction is great to set up – because it's paid off in about 15 years, it continues to grow even in a bad economy, and you're always covered no matter your health or age. You can start small ($50,000?) and can always buy more.

True Story - My Whole Life Insurance

I currently own several large, fully paid up (and growing) Whole Life insurance policies.

I purchased my first Whole Life insurance policy when I was 33 years old. I paid a total of $200K. My death benefit is 500% larger than my cost. I was single, started making good money and figured someday I'd have children - who'd listen to me if they had $ to inherit!

Even through periods of historically low interest rates and economic downturns my Whole Life policies have continued to pay dividends of between five and eight percent.

The dividends earned on these policies now completely pay for my annual insurance premiums plus purchase additional paid-up insurance. If you do choose to purchase a Whole Life insurance policy, verify the issuing insurance company is highly rated and has been in business for at least twenty years.

Links to life insurance company websites: www.FinancialBanana-Split.com

Moral of the Story

Planning for the future now, when things are generally cheaper, pays off.

Dealing with Documents

You need to retain certain documents to prove an event occurred, taxes were paid, repairs were done, items were purchased, donations were made, etc.

The IRS has the right to audit you going back three years . . . forever if they suspect fraud.

It's reasonable to keep all documents related to major purchases – life insurance, auto, appliances, electronics, etc., for at least seven years or longer if a warranty exists.

Common documents to retain include:

- Bank and securities statements, documents showing income, tax returns, wage and property tax statements.
- Birth certificate, passport, driver's license, social security card, automobile title, etc.
- Insurance policies, warranties, repair receipts, medical expenses.
- Charity and purchase receipts, registrations, manuals, deeds.

Store them in a secure, dry, and accessible place.

Your system can be as simple as keeping all documents for the same year in a plastic folder in a locked, fireproof cabinet.

The importance of document retention is multiplied when you have collaborative ownership (On website: Collaborate for Wealth Building). People count on you, and you count on them to be able to offer documented proof events occurred.

Original signed and dated documents offer the best proof. As added protection, take pictures and store data electronically.

Estate Planning

Your estate is created, after death, from your assets, including cash, securities, real estate, life insurance proceeds, jewelry, other personal assets, etc. You need a will and revocable trust. Your estate will be controlled, distributed, and assessed large fees by your state's probate court (and its attorneys) unless you have a revocable trust, as explained below:

Will: Your entire estate goes into probate court. You can name an Executor (financially settles your estate – court not obligated to obey) and appoint a guardian for your minor children. The court decides who gets what and when, including hearing petitions from relatives or others, and it decides guardianship.

Revocable Trust: The assets in this trust avoid probate court. You name an executor to distribute your estate according to your wishes.

Guardianship of minor children is still decided by the court. All major assets should be put into this trust. Minor assets and personal effects are distributed according to your will. You can modify or cancel a revocable trust anytime. Complete with attorney/service/on-line.

Your bank/financial accounts can also name a beneficiary(s) to avoid these assets from going into probate. Ask bank.

Documents can be prepared by an Attorney, a service or on-line.

Ingredient Four ⍰ Conclusion

This is the purpose of Avoiding Financial Landmines: to protect your money by understanding and implementing basics whose cost is small relative to what you've got to lose.

Ingredient Four: Major Points

1. Using basic financial tools: Income tax preparation/understanding contracts/Insurance/maintaining documents/estate planning - will protect your wealth from many potential legal and financial losses.
2. Income taxes: You need to compute and file every year using correct form: 1040EZ=Income below $100K and limited deductions /1040A= Income below $100K with mortgage-pension-loan deductions, etc./ 1040=income over $100K and deductions exceed standard deduction.
3. Definitions: Income tax=A tax on your earnings/Deductions= Amounts deducted from your income tax to reduce taxes owed/ Personal exemption=A specific amount allowed by the IRS/Tax credit: An amount deducted directly from your income tax owed/ Filing deadline: date tax return due/ Tax year=calendar year for most individual tax payers.

4. Contracts are legally binding documents: you follow their terms and conditions. Check contract for 10 points using 3-step review: payment requirements-non-compliance-termination-duration-performance required-returns-assignment-buy option-insurance requirements-best deal available.
5. Insurance protects your assets from being sold to cover losses.
6. Deductible: Amount you owe before insurance company pays. Carry insurance coverage at least equal to value of your assets.
7. Insurance: Term life =specific period / Whole life= in effect until death.
8. Retain certain documents: Bank and brokerage statements-major purchase receipts—insurance and medical policies—income tax returns.
9. Estate created after death. A Revocable Trust avoids Probate Court.
10. Understand your paycheck: withholding, deductions, etc.
11. Know your local taxes: Sales and property tax.
12. Know basic language and requirements for a contract and loan application.

5

Ingredient Five: Investing for Wealth and Early Retirement

Investing is the whipped cream in the banana split. Fund it after paying current necessities: food/rent/utilities/medical, etc. and fully funding your 4-month Emergency Fund for same.

Hierarchy of Money Flow

(Where to target your money)

1. Your Home – mortgage payoff or saving for a first home. (After you've funded your Emergency Fund = 4-months living necessities: food, rent, utilities, etc.).
2. Retirement – pension investments.
3. Retirement – non-pension investments.
4. Non-Retirement – monies you can afford to lose (Funny bone).

Implementing automatic deductions for the first three targets increases the probability you'll achieve financial success because, if you don't have the cash to spend, you won't spend it. It's basic "out of sight, out of mind" psychology. It works!

First Target Area - Your Home

The first target to aim your money at is your home or saving for your first home (collaborative or sole ownership) because a fully paid-for home is the foundation of the American Dream.

Your home is also your initial and primary investment because home price appreciation is a fundamental component of wealth creation (Ingredient Two).

All your basic costs of home ownership – principal + interest + taxes + insurance (PITI) – must be fully paid for every month to avoid foreclosure. If you're saving for a home, fund the two future home items in your monthly budget and add these to your savings account.

This is done before funding investments and pension(s) unless your employer matches pension contributions (see below).

Second Target Area - Pension(s)

The second target to aim your money at is your pension plan. This money grows tax free, or tax deferred, stimulating growth. Matching funds from your employer (if offered) is effectively free money (see pension details below).

Third Target Area - Investments

The third target to aim your money at is your non-pension investments. Income and gains generated are taxable when earned, but choosing solid investments and then reinvesting earnings back into these investments supercharges financial growth.

Fourth Target Area - Funny Bone

The fourth target to aim your money at is your funny bone. It's for enjoying and maybe learning something – about money and yourself.

I. Pension Plans

II. Investing:

a) Securities Primer: Stocks, Bonds, Mutual Funds, etc.

b) Classic Investing Strategies

c) How to Start Investing

III. Retirement Planning

I. Pension Plans

You need to understand your pension plan options – (I) the types of pensions and how they work, and (II) (III) how and where to invest pension monies etc. to maximize growth for early retirement.

Definition: Pension plans are used for accumulating money during your working years to support you financially in your retirement, post-working years.

Pensions maximize money by avoiding taxes during their growth years. Taxes are only paid when you take distributions – usually at retirement (for most pension types, see below). Your employer might even add to your pension contributions, up to a certain percentage, called employer "matching." Ask your employer.

Funding pensions should be done directly after fully paying your housing costs, especially where your employer matches pension contributions. This is free money you don't want to miss.

Pension plans are important if you want more money because they make and save you money in these important ways:

- Quicker growth – not impeded by taxes.

- Your employer's matching pension contribution equals free money (possibly even better than free ice cream).
- Pension plans save you money because you pay less tax. Certain pension contributions are deductible from income.

Pension Plans - Basic Mechanics

Sponsorship (management) of pension plans:

- 401(k) – Company as sponsor, regular and defined benefit pension plans. Company sets this up for you.
- IRA (Individual Retirement Account) – You as sponsor, traditional and Roth pension plans. Your bank can help you set this up – it's a very common service. Ask.

Who contributes and maximum amounts allowed:

- 401(k) – You, as employee, up to $20,500 annually (currently). The company might match your pension contributions.
- IRA – You, as individual, up to $7,000 annually (currently).

Federal income tax: Pension monies grow tax free or tax deferred.

- 401(k) – Contributions are deductible. Distributions are taxed at time taken out – at your then income tax rate.
- IRA (traditional) – Contributions are deductible. Distributions are taxed at time taken out – at your then income tax rate.
- IRA (Roth) – Contributions are not deductible. Distributions are not taxed because the money you contributed was already taxed as income when you earned it.

Additional Pension Information

- Payouts can be a set amount: 401(k) "defined benefit" plan.
- You can have a 401(k) and an IRA at the same time.

- A SEP plan is for self-employed persons.
- There are pension rules regarding loans, early withdrawals, allowable pension investments, etc.

Pension information: www.FinancialBananaSplit.com

Retirement and Pension Quotes

- "There's one thing I always wanted to do before I quit . . . retire!" (Groucho Marx, comedian)
- "I'm retired. Goodbye tension, hello pension!" (Anonymous)

II. a) Securities Primer: Stocks, Bonds, Mutual Funds, Etc.

1. **Securities:** Certificates of value – stock or bond - issued by an entity (company or government) denoting ownership in its assets (stock) or as a holder of its debt (bond). They are investment instruments. They fluctuate in value. Can be bought and sold.
2. **A Share of Stock:** A certificate of value issued by a company denoting the holder has an ownership interest in the company. It is an investment security. A stock may or may not be a dividend (cash) paying type. They fluctuate in value.
3. **Common Stock:** General class of stock issued by a company. Includes company voting rights.
4. **Preferred Stock:** A stock with a fixed dividend. No company voting rights. Its dividends get paid before common stock dividends.
5. **Bonds:** A debt certificate issued by a company or government. They pay interest income. Company issued = fully taxable. Federal govt. issued (Treasuries) = No state tax. State/city/ county issued (Muni) = No federal tax. Quality rated: A-B-C-D. Your interest

rate doesn't change. Bond values increase when Feds raise interest rates/ decline when lowered. Why? New bonds will have a higher or lower issue/stated interest rate than yours. This makes them more or less valuable than yours. Buyers pay a premium for higher rate / discount for lower rate.

6. **Stock Markets and Bond Markets:** Market places where stocks and bonds are listed and exchanged - bought and sold. Examples: Dow Jones Industrial Average (DJIA), Standard & Poor's 500 (S&P500) Nasdaq, S&Pglobal.com / moodys.com.
7. **Mutual Funds-ETF's-Index Funds:** These are bundles of securities each with their own objective: growth, income or both, etc. Mutual Funds trade at the end of the day, and are professionally managed for a fee. ETF's can be traded throughout the day as stocks and may or may not be managed. Index Funds track a particular market index and are not managed.
8. **Federal Reserve Bank (The "Fed"):** The central bank of the United States. It controls the economy's money supply-expands or contracts it-mainly by raising (contracts) or lowering (expands) interest rates. This affects interest rates on mortgages, loans and credit cards. The stock market generally rises during periods of monetary expansion and declines during contraction.
9. **Crypto Currency:** Electronic money created by and stored on computers. Not issued or supported by the U.S. Government. Highly volatile / risky. Bitcoin and Ethereum are examples.

II b) Classic Investing Strategies

I offer the following classic investing strategies not to make you an expert, but to give you familiarity with investing enough that you'll be able to do research and use the information presented throughout this book to make thoughtful investment choices, ones that power you towards the American Dream.

Speculating versus Investing

Want to achieve the American Dream? Then stick to investing your money, not speculating. Why?

A short-term investment (less than one year) is called speculating, and it is basically gambling. Why? In the short term, the markets don't necessarily reflect realistic values – prices are more emotionally driven. If you need to sell, you're risking selling at a loss.

A long-term investment (10 years or more) is called investing because it rides the wave of market fluctuations and generally returns to a realistic valuation. Use this for retirement savings.

Anything can happen at any time and a longer term tends to smooth things out. The typical economic cycle usually lasts about 12 years from Good > Bad > Good. Investing uses the long term as leverage to grow. Speculating does not – it gambles on a quick profit.

Want to practice speculating or investing without using real money? Find real-time market play at www.FinancialBananaSplit.com.

How's the Weather?

Want to achieve the American Dream? Then make a little effort to understand what you're buying before you buy it.

If you were considering relocating, you'd gather basic information about the new area before deciding to move there, such as:

• Year-round climate • Housing costs • Cost-of-living • School quality • Employment opportunities • Recreation • Shopping, etc.

Before buying securities also gather some basic information:

Individual Stocks and Stock Funds

- Cost to buy = NAV (Net Asset Value).
- Cost to own = Expense Ratio: Equal to a % such as .45, .07, 1.2, etc. Includes all fees + front or back-load charges (escape charges). Broker's managed account fee (if any) is in addition to these.
- Only buy No-load funds: Mutual/ETF/Index.
- Quality rating per independent rating agencies: Morningstar, etc.
- Price volatility history (ups + downs) vs. stock market/peers/index.
- Current and historical P/E ratios for stock / fund.
- Who holds stocks/funds? Which brokerage? How insured? Limit?
- Ability to buy/sell and cost to do so (transaction fee, etc.).
- Compare all above elements to other same-type stocks/funds.
- In-depth review - page 121: Fundamental and Technical Analysis.
- Dividends paid? Amount? Frequency? History? Taxable status?

Individual Bonds and Bond Funds

All above information for individual stocks and funds, plus:

• Check quality rating: A-B-C-D. Investment grade = Baa/BBB. • Lower rating pays higher interest rate but involves more risk. • Effective (actual) interest rate you'll receive after expenses? • Tax structure: Subject to federal + state income tax? Both/one/none? • Compare your yield to current 10-year Treasury. Higher = more risk.

Plan and Goal

Want to achieve the American Dream? Then you need a plan and a goal. A plan is for taking steps. A goal is what you measure your steps against (progress). A plan can be simple. The most important parts are starting and following it.

Your plan needs to be flexible to account for unforeseeable changes while still continuing towards your goal. Example: Goal – Save $1,800 in one year. Plan – Set up an automatic transfer with my bank for $150 per month from my checking to my savings account. Add extra money when available in case one month a financial emergency prevents me from contributing.

Risk versus Return

Want to achieve the American Dream? Then how much risk or loss are you willing to take for a higher return? This is the basic question of risk versus return. You only take more risk because you expect a greater or better outcome than from a less risky investment. It's foolish to put your money at high risk. Save gambling for Las Vegas, where your odds are probably better and casinos bring you free drinks. Gamble only with what you can afford to lose, not with your housing, savings, or retirement money.

The higher your risk, the higher your return should be.

Current P/E compared to historic P/E indicates risk (see below).

Price-to-Earnings Ratio (P/E Ratio)

Want to achieve the American Dream? Then understand at what price you should buy a security or fund. Buy low, sell high = faster wealth. How? Calculate it's "P/E Ratio" = Price to Earnings Ratio. This number tells you a security's risk relative to its price history. It's a good indicator of how low and how high it can go over time. P/E Ratio = The current price of a security divided by its earnings per share (EPS). Example: Stock price = $60. EPS = $5. $60 / $5 = 12. It's P/E ratio = 12. Does a P/E ratio of 12 make this a high or low risk to buy at this time? Compare to historical P/E found on the company's website and at www.FinancialBananaSplit.com. The S&P 500 historically returns to a P/E Ratio of 16, a neutral buy. It's moved between a P/E ratio low of 6 (1949) and a high of 120 (2001, the ".com" boom) Where is it today? I wish I had known this simple information years ago! My loss, your gain.

Multiple Income Streams

Want to achieve the American Dream? Then understand and develop multiple income streams. This refers to income from multiple sources, which can include job salary, income from rental properties, investment income, hobby income, part-time job income, your own business, etc. Use extra income for investing and new cash flow areas. The goal is early retirement with multiple income streams.

Automatic Deductions

Want to achieve the American Dream? Then use this "set it and forget it" method to grow your money. Monies directed by you to be automatically deducted from a paycheck or bank account to be put into savings/pension/ investment accounts are automatic deductions. This supports the "out of sight, out of mind" concept and is a stepping stone on the path to the American Dream. If the contribution to your pension, house down payment, mortgage, investments, etc. is deducted from your paycheck before you ever see it, then you don't miss it. You'll automatically adjust your lifestyle and budget to fit.

Pay Yourself First

Want to achieve the American Dream? Then choose investments that reinvest income or pay you directly instead of receiving nothing. When purchasing securities, this refers to only buying securities that pay dividends or interest. You're investing and risking your money. Shouldn't you get paid for it? Some investors believe companies that pay dividends are more trustworthy because they always need to insure a good cash flow. This way, they can always pay shareholder dividends. This makes them potentially less risky investments. You receive dividends even if your securities have gone down in value. This helps steady emotions during market ups and downs (volatility).

True Story - Dividends

A few years ago, I bought shares of a mutual fund at $12 per share. It paid a 7.25% federal tax-free dividend income on my principal investment. Due to economic variables (none affected the ability of this fund to generate its dividend) its price fell 66% to four dollars per share. They paid their dividend like "clockwork" – on time and exactly to the penny – even though the fund lost two-thirds of its market value.

It was a rough ride emotionally, but I didn't sell and continued to collect my dividends.

Several months later the fund reversed its downward trend and went up 50%, again due to market variables having nothing to do with the financial health of the fund itself. I was receiving income while owning the fund through a volatile period. It kept me from selling for a loss, which would have been a big mistake. Funds list: www.financialbananasplit.com

Dollar Cost Averaging

Want to achieve the American Dream? Then follow a steady, long-term investing schedule. This means buying the same dollar amount of the same security each period as set by you: monthly, quarterly, annually, on your birthday, your pet's birthday, etc. Sometimes it's expensive and sometimes it's cheap . . . It all averages out over time. This has proven better than trying to time the market.

Example: You buy 10 shares of XYZ Corporation stock every year on your birthday. One year, a share can cost $92. Another year, it might cost $121. Do this for twenty years, and your average price might be $106. You didn't over or underpay: the average price you paid is called "Goldilocks" – it's just right.

Buy and Hold

Want to achieve the American Dream? Then choose quality, believe in it, and never let it go. (Gee, too bad we don't apply this strategy to choosing friends.) This means buying and never selling high-quality securities, whether bought as individual stocks or as a fund – you would keep the fund if it were highly rated* overall.

*Highly rated with a long history of dividend or interest payments. Large, well-know, high-quality, dividend-paying companies such as IBM, McDonalds, Walmart, Johnson & Johnson and Colgate Palmolive. Their known as Dividend Aristocrats. Funds: VOO// NOBL/REGL.

Buying and selling what you hope is the next "hot" stock involves higher risk by trying to time the market. This reduces long-term returns by incurring broker fees and other charges each time you buy or sell and losses if you guess wrong.

Diversification

Want to achieve the American Dream? Then lower your investment risk by diversifying. This means owning different types (classes) of assets: stocks, bonds, commodities, and real estate. Owning a home is your primary real estate investment, so you're basically covered for this. All investments go up and down unpredictably over time: When one is up, another is down.

Familiar with the carnival game where you hammer a mole? Diversification is the same concept: You never know which mole is going to pop up, but if you place the same bet on all of them at the same time, you always pick a winner.

The balanced mutual fund is an example of diversification. These funds are also known as "all in one" investments because they hold a diversified group of assets: stocks, bonds, etc. Fund examples: VBIAX/FFFGX/ONGAX.

Target Funds

Want to achieve the American Dream? Then don't pick securities – let a target fund do it for you. With these funds you pick your expected year of retirement and the fund automatically adjusts its mix of stocks and bonds as you reach your retirement age. It has more stocks for growth in the early years and more bonds for income payout in your later, retirement years. Target mutual funds - 2060 retirement date – examples include: VTTSX/FDKLX/SSDYX.

The Rule of 72

Want to achieve the American Dream? Then know how long it takes for your investment to double. This formula shows the number of years it takes an investment to double at an estimated growth rate or "yield" (through appreciation, dividends, interest, or a combination thereof) using reinvesting. You simply divide 72 by your expected annual yield.

Example: You invest $2,000, which pays an annual dividend of 8%. Then: 72 ÷ 8% = 9. It takes nine years for your money to double at an 8% yield with all dividends and interest reinvested.

Stock "Splits"

Want to achieve the American Dream? Then understand this basic mechanism of how stocks work. A stock "split" is when a company's stock price has reached a high price and the company splits its stock: It gives its shareholders two (or more) shares of half-valued stock for every one share they own. Split shares historically rise in value.

Compounding

Want to achieve the American Dream? Then understand and use this time-tested wealth creator. The most powerful element in wealth creation is ***TIME.*** This is best illustrated by the compounding effect. (Non-pension and non-ETF gains are passed-thru and taxable).

Compounding means growth by reinvesting dividends and interest back into the securities that produced them.

This especially applies to pensions, where income isn't taxed. Your money grows fast because you're receiving income on your reinvestment as well as income on your original investment. Simple interest grows money slower. You only receive income on your original investment, not again on the income it generates.

Equation - Simple vs. Compound Interest

This equation shows compound interest rate growth to be triple that of simple interest rate growth: simple interest: 3 + 3 + 3 = 9 vs. compound interest: 3 x 3 x 3 = 27.

A compound vs. simple interest rate graph is illustrated below:

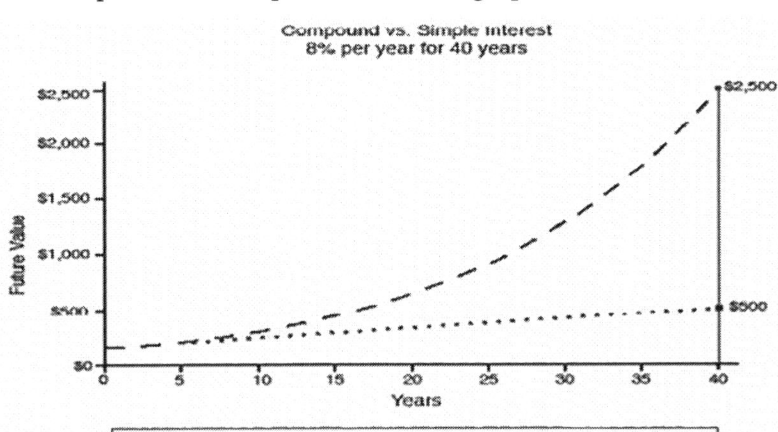

As you can see, compound interest produced a result 500% greater ($500 vs $2,500) than simple interest.

Here's a pie chart with another way to view compound interest:

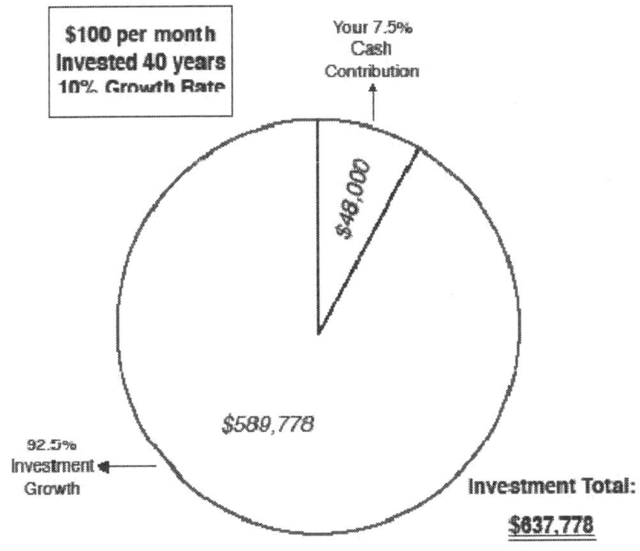

This shows $100 a month ($3.34 a day) invested for forty years in an S&P 500 index pension fund. This fund has historically earned 10% per year with reinvested dividends, which is the basis of compounding. Your total contributions of $48,000 grows to $637,778.

You contributed 7.5%. Compound growth contributed 92.5%.

Think of it as: Simple + Easy = Millionaire.

True Story - June Chopper and Compound Interest

A friend of mine from the Midwest (I call her June Chopper after the iconic mother character in a 1950s television show) was able to retire early, and both she and her husband (ex) were able to accumulate over a combined one million dollars.

How? They were middle-class working people who, through steady automatic deductions into their pension plans and leaving their monies untouched, let their investments grow through compound interest – earning interest on the interest their investments produced and then reinvesting it.

She used part of this money to buy a house – cheap – for her daughter during the housing meltdown of 2008 – another smart financial move. She did good, and now the market value of the house is almost triple what she paid for it. It's the "buy low, sell high" technique and mindset.

This story proves average income earners have a very real shot at financial independence. It just takes patience and following the basic strategies provided throughout this book.

An Easy-to-Learn Tasty Anagram

I = Interest
C = Compounding
E = Everyday
C = Creates
R = Real
E = Easy
A = Additional
M = Money

Illustration from the board game
Ice Cream and Money ... For Everybody!

THINK
I-C-E C-R-E-A-M
GROW RICH

Go to www.FinancialBananaSplit.com
to buy this board game.

II(c) How to Start Investing A Simple, Time-tested Investment Strategy

The performance standard against which most investments are measured is the S&P 500 (Standard & Poor's). It contains five hundred of the largest companies listed on the NYSE and NASDAQ stock market exchanges. It represents 75% of the US economy.

A basic investment strategy is to buy two low-fee, broad-based market ETF index funds: one for stocks and one for bonds.

Example: You buy one share of each type of ETF: stock-VOO @$377 and bond-BND@$76.

A classic money ratio is 3/4 (75%) stocks, 1/4(25%) bonds. In the above example, buying an even number of stock and bond shares would give you 83% stocks, 17% bonds. Simple. This is within reasonable range of the classic stock/bond ratio. This strategy isn't perfect, but there's a thousand worse ones.

To do this, simply open a brokerage account (detailed below) with written instructions to buy per the example above. Fund it with automatic deductions from your paycheck or checking account – after paying all housing costs and pension contributions matched by your employer. This is how you fund your IRA.

Review all investments at least every month to become comfortable with your brokerage statement and make sure you understand all charges and fees.

Easy: Opening Your Own Brokerage Account

Want to achieve the American Dream? It's time for you to open a brokerage account.

1. Open a brokerage account with your bank or online with a low-cost brokerage: Vanguard, Fidelity, TD Ameritrade, Charles Schwab. All are good choices. Compare costs for fees, trading, balance requirements, etc. Www.FinancialBananaSplit.com for links to websites.
2. Specify that you want all interest and dividends generated from your investments to be reinvested. This is the basis of compounding, the way to supercharge investment growth.
3. Open a Roth IRA pension account where you opened your brokerage account. Use this for brokerage securities up to

allowed limit. This allows faster growth because it grows free of taxes. Note: You can set up a Roth IRA as an individual even if you already have a company pension plan. You would contribute money into your company's pension plan before this Roth IRA, at least up to your employer's match.

4. Select a fund from the list of balanced funds, an S&P 500 index ETF fund, a mutual fund, or the broad stock market and bond index funds (Vanguard or similar low-cost funds) noted. Instruct your broker which investments to purchase and when.
5. Set up a monthly automatic deduction from your checking account or paycheck to go directly into this pension account, as much as you can budget.
6. Review your investment regularly to determine its relative performance before buying or selling. See www.FinancialBananaSplit.com for comparisons.
7. Increase your monthly contribution as you are able.
8. Enjoy a nice, early retirement. Buy me a drink when we meet at the cruise ship bar – thanks!

A new type of automated investment service is also available. It's low cost and uses sophisticated mathematics to invest your money in domestic and international stocks and bonds. It's based on your answers to their questionnaire.

Apps to assist with investing are also on brokerage websites. See www.FinancialBananaSplit.com for website links.

True Story - Pat

Let's revisit the successful investor equation:

Simple + Easy = Millionaire

Here's a real-life investment story from my tennis buddy, Pat. Pat went from complex to simple investing and bought this new sports car to celebrate his good decisions and fortune.

Pat is a smart, educated computer engineer in his 60s. He has a good income and lives a comfortable life.

He invested his money with a traditional full-service brokerage firm, paying them about 1.5% annually in fees plus other costs. Even though he'd had his money in the financial markets for decades, Pat never saw his financial picture significantly improve.

After losing much of his portfolio value in the 2001 financial crash, Pat decided to take what was left of his investments and transfer them into a low-cost S&P 500 index fund with Vanguard Brokerage Services.

I met Pat in 2014 at our local tennis group and immediately noticed his brand-new European sports car. I told him I admired his car, and he told me his investment story.

With his own investments under his own control, Pat doubled his money as he rode the rising tide of a recovering market. Pat's success is a real-life story of the investment equation:

Simple + Easy = Millionaire. It works!

Should You Hire an Investment Advisor? Pros and Cons

Want to achieve the American Dream? Here's two **secrets** for successful money management whether you decide to use an investment advisor or not:

1. You must know the basics of financial investing.
2. You must develop a healthy relationship with money.

Why? Because you need to track and understand why your investments are performing the way they are whether you're working with an investment advisor or not.

Knowing this helps you see the bad times with an understanding of why it happened and calculating when it will turn around instead of "why, poor little me," panicking and selling at the low point (been there, done that).

Fortunately, these two secrets for successful money management are explored and explained on our website section: Gain Money Self-Awareness and in this book: Achieve Financial Literacy.

After you've read and understood this book's information, consider these additional points to help you decide if a financial advisor – and which type – is right for you:

- Don't hire a financial advisor to assist you if you only own "set it and forget it" S&P 500 and bond index funds. Just set it up and use a discount broker.
- Most discount brokers now offer low-cost "over the phone" services if you need to consult with a financial broker and "robot" broker services that take into account your risk tolerance and correct for market fluctuations using math algorithms.

- A full-service advisor's best use is for investors who actively trade and/or people with more complex financial situations.
- If you don't want to handle your money for whatever reason, use a financial advisor. Consider putting at least part of your investments into a simple S&P 500 stock index and ETF bond fund in a 3:1 ratio with a discount broker. These funds should not be in your broker's "managed" account, because you're charged an additional fee for this.
- Track your broker's performance against the above funds over the long term and in consideration of major market fluctuations. This really helps you understand the markets. Your broker should help you with adjusting your financial mix to soften losses and take advantage of opportunities. Talk!
- What do I do? I use a Vanguard brokerage services low-cost S&P 500 index fund as well as a financial advisor. However, the funds I have with my financial advisor are specialty municipal bond and energy funds – federally tax free. I don't pay him an additional fee for these. The funds pay him a 12B-1 fee, which is already built into their expenses. They can fluctuate wildly, but I understand the risks and like the steady income (cash flow rocks!).

III Retirement Planning

Your retirement years focus is the opposite of your working years saving and investing focus. During your working years it's how much can I make. During retirement it's how much can I take.

The information learned in Ingredient Five can be applied to retirement planning because your investments still need to generate money – now more for income than growth. Once again, it's all about cash flow.

Calculating Your Retirement Budget

Complete your monthly budget on page 17. Use amounts relevant to your retirement years as follows:

Income – All items net of taxes: social security, pensions – including required distributions – estimated net income during retirement from part-time jobs, rental income, annuities, investments, etc.

Note: A "4% rule" is intended as the maximum amount you should withdraw per year in order to have your investments be a source of income until your death. More than this might require lowering expenses or increasing income.

Expenses – Your monthly expenses for housing will be much lower if you live in your home and have paid off its mortgage.

To better estimate general costs during retirement (food, utilities, etc.), account for inflation by adding 4% to your current budget expenses (for relevant items) each year between now and the year you'll turn 75. It's just a "guesstimate" based on average longevity.

Current age = 35. Years, until age 75 = 40.

Therefore: 4% x 40 years = 160%. Add 160% to each expense.

A Current $300 expense item + 160% =$780.

Annuities

Annuities are life insurance company financial contracts. They're a combination of securities and life insurance with a minimum guaranteed income.

They're popular for retirement planning because the guaranteed monthly payouts might be more than you can comfortably withdraw from your investments over a long retirement period.

Annuities can be costly and complex, and you pay big commissions to brokers. They have high operating expenses and steep surrender charges (if you stop paying).

How do you buy the most cost-efficient annuities? Source: Directly from the issuing insurance company.

Type: SPIA (single premium immediate annuity). Why? You pay a one-time lump sum to the insurance company. This removes your risk of policy cancellation for non-payment. A fixed-payout annuity is more reliable than one with a variable payout. See what death benefit, if any, your contract pays. www.FinancialBananaSplit.com for annuity websites. Purchasing separate investments and life insurance is an option.

Kid Stuff

Investment information is also applicable to children. The Uniform Gift to Minors Act (UGMA) allows an adult to open a separate investment account for a minor and control it until the minor achieves majority age. It can be opened at most financial institutions – I opened a UGMA for my son. With investing, time is power and children have the longest investment timeline. Coverdale and 529 Savings Plans are other options. These programs are more structured/restricted to funding education.

Ingredient Five - Conclusion

Investing for wealth and early retirement isn't magic. The conditions to achieve your goals occur around us every day. Understand and apply the information in this Ingredient to use these conditions to your maximum financial benefit.

Ingredient Five: Major Points

1. Target your money: Emergency Fund > Mortgage/Down Payment > Pension > Non-Pension Investments > Funny-Bone.
2. A pension is for saving money during work>living on in retirement. Pension investment growth is fast, not slowed by taxes.
3. Basic Securities= stocks & bonds. Stocks = growth & dividend income. Bonds=interest income and are usually less risky than stocks but less growth (worth) potential.
4. Mutual Funds/ETF's/ Index Funds own many different securities=less risk than any single security.
5. Investing = holding securities long-term. Speculating = gambling (holding a security for less than one year).
6. Have a realistic investment goal and a basic plan to fund it.
7. Definitions: P/E ratio= stock price divided by earnings per share. S&P 500 neutral risk=16/Multiple Income Stream=Salary + investment income + rental income, etc./ Pay Yourself First=only buying stocks which pay dividends/ Dollar Cost Averaging=buying the same dollar amount of the same stock over time/Buy and Hold=buying quality stocks for the long term/ Diversification=owning different classes of assets: Stocks-bonds-real estate/Rule of 72=divide 72 by annual return rate = # years for security to double with reinvestment/ Stock Split=receiving 2 shares equal in value to your one share/ Compound Interest=fast growth by reinvesting stock dividends to buy more stock/ Classic Investment Strategy=75%stocks + 25%bonds/Open your own discount brokerage account without managed fees/An annuity is an

investment combination of life insurance and securities/4% Rule=don't take more than 4% of your investments a year so they last through retirement/A UGMA -Uniform Gift to Minors Act= adult can open investment account for minor.

8. Additional Important Financial Information: REIT/Contra Assets/Leveraging/Long + Short Selling/Social Security/Medicare/FICA/Mutual Funds vs. ETF Taxes/Growth + Income Securities/ Stock Options/Large + Small Cap./Junk Bonds/ Inheritance/Capital Assets: Duration-Gain-Loss-Taxes/TIPS/ Market Sectors
9. Securities Primer: Securities/A Share of Stock/Common Stock/ Preferred Stock/ A Bond/Stock Markets and Bond Markets/ Mutual Funds-ETF's-Index Funds/Federal Reserve Bank (The "Fed") / Crypto Currency

Additional Important Financial Information

1. **REIT**- Real Estate Investment Trust: A stock company that owns, operates or finances real estate. It might own actual real estate or only trade mortgages.
2. **CONTRA - ASSETS**: Investments whose rise or fall in value do not follow the stock market. Their value might go in the opposite direction. Gold is the classic contra asset. Its value generally rises when stock markets have large declines.
3. **LEVERAGING**: Using other peoples or an entity's money to help you purchase an asset. Example: House mortgage. Your 20% down payment. Bank lends 80%.
4. **LONG and SHORT SELLING**: Long position – you purchase a contract today for a stock you hope will go up in the future. Short position – you purchase a contract today for a stock you hope will go down in the future. Profit if you're right, loss if wrong.
5. **SOCIAL SECURITY**: A federal insurance program paying monthly cash benefits to persons 62 and older who have paid into the program through payroll tax deductions.
6. **MEDICARE**: A federal medical insurance program mainly for those 65 years of age and older who have paid into the program by payroll taxes.
7. **FICA**: A federal payroll tax which supports Social Security and Medicare benefits.
8. **MUTUAL FUNDS VS ETF'S: TAX DIFFERENCE:** Mutual Fund: You pay taxes on the fund's reported gains while you own the fund but don't actually receive these gains until you sell your shares. ETF's: Gains only reported/taxed when you sell. No taxes paid on gains until distributed in either type if in a pension account.

9. **GROWTH STOCKS:** Bought to (hopefully) outperform the market. Dividend income not a focus. Usually high P/E ratio. More risk implied.
10. **VALUE STOCKS:** Bought for dividend income and to keep pace with the market. Usually low P/E ratio. Less risk implied
11. **STOCK OPTIONS:** Gives you the right, not obligation, to buy or sell a stock on a certain date/certain price. Put=bet stock will be lower/Call=bet stock will be higher.
12. **LARGE CAP/ SMALL CAP:** Refers to a company's capitalization /market value: (# of outstanding shares) x (current share price).
13. **JUNK BONDS:** Bonds rated below investment grade (BBA or lower). Higher interest/higher risk. Funds: JNK/DLHYX/SJB.
14. **INHERITANCE:** a) There is no federal inheritance tax. Six states impose an inheritance tax: IA/KY/MD/NE/NJ/PA. b) An estate pays a federal estate tax if it exceeds $12 million. Thirteen states impose an estate tax: HI/IL/MD/MA/MI/NY/OR/RI/VT/WA/DC. c) Life insurance proceeds are not taxed. d) Distributions taken by you after inheriting a 401K pension are taxable to you. No tax if it's a Roth pension. e) Other assets: House and valuables (art, auto, etc.) are subject to capital gains tax when you sell them if your selling price exceeds their market value at the time you inherited them. f) Assets put into a Trust before death avoids probate court.

    What to do with inherited money? Inherited funds would be directed into the Hierarchy of Money Flow, as detailed in Ingredient Five. A large investible amount might be a good candidate for Dollar Cost Averaging so you don't invest everything at once. Put the money to be invested later in a savings, money market or CD per Ingredient One.

15. **CAPITAL ASSETS: DURATION-GAINS-LOSSES-TAXES**

CAPITAL ASSETS: Most common are real estate and securities.

LONG-TERM CAPITAL ASSET: Asset held over one year.

SHORT-TERM CAPITAL ASSET: Asset held under one year.

LONG-TERM CAPITAL GAIN: Sale of a long-term asset: tax 15%.

SHORT-TERM CAPITAL GAIN: Sale of a short-term asset. Taxed as ordinary income.

Capital gains and losses are netted against each other within a tax year. Excess capital losses can be deducted from ordinary income in current and future years at max $3,000 per year and can also be carried-over to deduct against future capital gains. Specific tax rules apply to real estate, crypto, high-income earners, etc.

16. **TREASURY INFLATION PROTECTED SECURITIES (T.I.P.S.):** These are government bonds issued by the Federal Department of the Treasury. Their value and interest payments are adjusted 2x per year to track the consumer price index of inflation as measured by the U.S. Bureau of Labor Statistics. They can be purchased at treasurydirect.gov or a participating bank.

17. **STOCK MARKET SECTORS:** The U.S. stock market can be divided into eleven financial sectors (categories) for convenience and understanding, as follows:

1. Healthcare 2. Materials 3. Real Estate 4. Consumer staples 5. Consumer Discretionary 6. Utilities 7. Energy 8. Industrials 9. Financials 10. Technology 11. Telecommunications.

The companies in a sector generally move in the same direction in response to overall market conditions. Each sector can be purchased as an ETF from brokerages.

18. **FINANCIAL ADVISOR SELECTION & LICENSE CHECK:** Selection: www.Letsmakeaplan.org. Or a bank/on-line, etc. Licensing: www.Brokercheck.finra.org Tel: (800) 289-9999. Important: Understand broker's fee/commission structure.
19. **REBALANCING:** The practice of selling best performing securities in your portfolio and buying yet-to-rise securities. Equals: Buy low/Sell high.
20. **INFLATION:** A general economy-wide increase in prices which causes a decrease in your purchasing power. This means the same things cost more to buy which indicates your money has lost value equal to the rate of inflation. Historically 3% annual rise.
21. **QUALIFIED DIVIDENDS:** Dividend income issued by a company whose stock you've owned 61+ days. It's taxed at long-term capital gains rates.
22. **SECURITES TAX FORM(s) 1099:** Issued annually by companies/govt. for: capital gains, interest income, dividends. Include with annual tax return(s).
23. **A PROSPECTUS:** A legal document filed with the SEC by a publicly held stock company/fund disclosing full details of its goals/risks/strategy.
24. **BEAR & BULL STOCK MARKETS:** Bear = When a Bull market declines 20% or more from height. Bull = When a Bear market rises 40% from low.
25. **ETHICAL INVESTING:** Socially Responsible (SRI), Biblically Responsible (BRI), Environmental-Social-Governance (ESG). Do basic financial reviews.
26. **FINTECH:** Technology to support/improve financial services-on-line, etc.

27. **F.I.R.E.** Financially Independent Retire Early movement. Basically living frugally. Home ownership helps get you there quicker, per this book.
28. **FUNDAMENTAL ANALYSIS:** To assess the financial health of a company by reviewing its financial statements: Balance Sheet, Income Statement, etc.
29. **TECHNICAL ANALYSIS:** Determining the probability a stock's value will increase/decrease based on market trends/patterns which affect that stock.

6

Ingredient Six: Goodwill and Charity

Goodwill and Charity are the cherry on top of the banana split. Its concentrated sweetness gives you purpose and helps direct resources so you feel good about your increasing wealth.

Sir Isaac Newton, Money, and Universal Truth

"For every action, there is an equal and opposite reaction."
"Everything in the Universe is connected."
(Sir Isaac Newton, English scientist, 17th C.)

Newton's Mathematical Principles of Natural Philosophy can be understood relative to our own actions: We generate energy and interact with all other energy in the universe. Newton proved that the amount of energy a body gives is equal to the amount of energy a body receives. This is known as a "universal truth." It applies at all times.

Example: "Where there's water, there's life." Astronomers look for evidence of water on planets because, if they find it, they know some form of life can/does/did exist there.

Newton's discovery was noted as visible motion. Everything in our universe has an energy component whether the source is purely physical, as in his famous gravity event – an apple falling from a tree – or thinking, which causes our brains to use electrical energy.

Example: Energy used for thinking can be transferred to and interact with external energy, as proven in a mind-only controlled drone race at a university. They used EEG (electroencephalogram) headsets powered by student brain waves (Cuthbertson 2016).

Money, goodwill, and charity also seem to be connected by universal energy. When you view and respect your money as energy, you pay attention to it and keep it under control, in order. The universe has order, and so should your money.

Putting money in order means accounting for and managing its inflow and outflow (energy = cashflow). This is consistent with the information on our website in Gain Money Self-Awareness..

Review on our website: Gain Money Self-Awareness, to understand your current relationship to money and how it can evolve to be consistent and balanced.

What you do with your money, intentions and actions, all have an energy flow.

Contributing to worthy charities, people, and causes with good intentions (and not because you feel obligated or because it makes you feel better than someone else) generates positive energy. Somehow the universe "gets it," and the energy you receive back is equal and positive. The federal government "gets it" too: charitable donations are deductible from income. This lowers your income tax liability thus increasing your cash flow.

The result is often more money. How? I don't know, but in this world, money seems to follow money.

True Story - Son's School

My son's school was seeking donations for new kitchen equipment. (In public schools, education budgets are limited.) One of the things needing replacement was a commercial dishwasher for $3,000. A grant paid for half.

My son is thriving. He has new friends and a B+ average – much higher than in his previous school where he was in danger of failing. And he's graduating high school one year early! Since parental joy is priceless, I decided to help out financially. I donated $1500 for the dishwasher. OK, so that's that, and I felt good about my donation.

At the same time, I decided to renovate my first-floor bathroom. I had a plumbing estimate for $4,000. The estimate seemed high, so I sought other bids. I looked on the internet and made several calls to local plumbers, but none returned my calls. I thought I would have to go with the original estimate.

When I was dropping my son off at school, I noticed there was a plumbing contractor close by. I decided I had nothing to lose and might as well walk in and see if they were interested. Wow! For the exact same job, they estimated $1,850. I saved over $2,000 and the only reason I found them was because they were next to my son's school. I saved much more than my donation amount.

I don't know if it was coincidence, Sir Isaac Newton, the Universe, or Spiritual influence but giving, goodwill, and charity seems to be consistent with positive outcomes in life. Ratings for charities: www.Charitynavigator.org

Ingredient Six - Conclusion

Goodwill and Charity can be thought of as: "Whatever good things we build end up building us." (Jim Rohn). Understand and apply the information in this Ingredient to help you put good energy into our world for a beneficial "boomerang" return.

> *"Service to others is the rent you pay*
> *for your room here on earth."*
> —Muhammad Ali

Conclusion

I sincerely hope you've found this book informative and will use it to create your own path to prosperity. It's a basic tool to use along the way.

Use it as a reference to evaluate your future financial options and strategies by comparing what's being offered and available to the fundamentals mentioned in these pages.

Do not make financial decisions until you fully understand the risks and rewards involved. Your questions are a powerful tool to help you gain this understanding.

Remember: If you can't explain it to someone in 3 sentences (an elevator pitch) you don't fully understand it yourself.

Happy reading, learning and achieving the American Dream!

The Board Game

BUY IT – PLAY IT – LEARN IT – EARN IT !

www.FinancialBananaSplit.com

Note To Educators and Lesson Planning Guide

Invite local professionals from various disciplines to speak. This will enhance and reinforce learning by bringing experiences from "real world" professionals into the classroom:

1. Real Estate Agent – Property evaluation and purchase.
2. Mortgage Broker – Mortgages: qualifying and types.
3. Banker – Bank services: opening and managing accounts.
4. Insurance Agent – Insurance purpose: types and function.
5. Financial Planner – Investing: basics and strategies.
6. Non-profit Representative – Charity: purpose and goals.
7. Social Worker/Psychologist – self-awareness and emotional control.
8. Communications/Media Professional – communication awareness and control.
9. Accountant (CPA) – Tax preparation, filing, and planning.
10. Author/Writing Coach – To enhance self-expression.

Note: A free classroom lesson planning guide for this book, including a sample test, available at: www.FinancialBananaSplit.com Tests

Bibliography And Further Reading

Bogar, Dawn. *The ABC's of Self.* Florida: ABC's of Self Inc. Publishing, 2013.

Berne, Eric, MD. *Games People Play: The Basic Handbook of Transactional Analysis.* New York: Ballantine Books, 1964.

Cuthbertson, Anthony. "Watch: World's First Mind-Controlled Drone Race. *Newsweek.* April 25, 2016.

Capacchione, Lucia, PhD. *Recovery of Your Inner Child.* New York: Simon & Schuster, 1991.

McKay, M., PhD, M. Davis, PhD, and P. Fanning. *Messages: The Communication Skills Book.* Oakland: New Harbinger Publications, 2009.

Orsi, J. and Doskow, E. *The Sharing Solution.* Berkeley: NOLO Publishing, 2009.

Orman, Suze. The 9 Steps to Financial Freedom. New York: Three Rivers Press, 1997.

Vanguard Brokerage Services, Valley Forge, PA 19482

Further Reading

www.FinancalBananaSplit.com

Acknowledgements

Many thanks to the people who directly or indirectly helped me on my journey of writing and completing this book:

- Professor Patrick Tierney, Palm Beach State College, FL, whose creative writing class ignited my passion for writing.
- The students in the above class who, although I was somewhere between their fathers' and grandfathers' ages, accepted me as their peer and showed me kindness and encouragement.
- Dawn Bogar, author of *The ABC'S of Self* (2013). She was a catalyst in my decision to write my own book. ("If she can do it, I can do it.")
- Rachel Weaver, author of *Point of Direction* (2014). Her critique classes improved my writing skills and book focus. She recommended my first editor and enabled me to meet my main financial critique editor.
- Editors Jennifer Phelps and Lind Stirling, who helped me improve my book to the point where it's hopefully useful, readable, and able to find an audience.

- Dave Schneller, financial critic and retired banker, who took pity on me as a novice writer of finance. Without his constant interest, I might have given up.
- Taylor Hilberry for graphic illustrations and Scott Charles for charts.
- My son, Adam, for being a soundboard to my many fragmented ideas, helping sort out the necessary from the nonsense.
- Book formatting by: Ghislain Viau, Creative Publishing Book Design. www.creativepublishingdesign.com

About The Author

Being raised and having had a successful multi-business career in New York City, the author, his son Adam (A decorated combat veteran), their dog, "Spikey", along with their 1972 Jaguar E-type, reside in state income-tax free Florida.

Mr. Rowland will continue to explore options for best communicating personal finance matters and related areas, in various formats, for all those who may benefit from a greater understanding in this arena.

Made in the USA
Columbia, SC
20 December 2022